Susan Dowell was born in London, educated there and at Sheffield University. She has lived in Ethiopia and Zambia, where she worked as a teacher and broadcaster. She is the co-author, with Linda Hurcombe, of *Dispossessed Daughters of Eve; Faith and Feminism* (1981) and has contributed to a number of collections on peace and feminism, including Virago's *Very Heaven: Women's Lives in the 60s* (1988). Her book *They Two Shall Be One; Monogamy in History and Religion* was published by HarperCollins in 1990. Married (to an Anglican priest) with four grown-up children she now lives in rural Shropshire.

Jane Williams was born and brought up in India. She is one of five sisters and spent most of her school years in single-sex boarding schools, so her horizons have always been dominated by 'women's issues'. She grew up in the Anglican Church, only noticing its sexism when the first measure to allow women to be priests was voted down. She read theology at Cambridge, and has served on Church commissions on the Doctrine of the Trinity and the Role of Bishops. She has written and taught on a wide variety of theological topics, many of them connected with women in the Christian tradition. She is married with one daughter.

BREAD, WINE & WOMEN

The Ordination Debate in the Church of England

SUSAN DOWELL
& JANE WILLIAMS

Published by VIRAGO PRESS Limited 1994
42–43 Gloucester Crescent, London NW1 7PD

Typeset by Florencetype Ltd, Kewstoke, Avon
Printed in Great Britain by Cox & Wyman Ltd,
Reading, Berkshire

CONTENTS

Preface

*I stand before Synod today as one who in her own
best judgement believes that she might be called to be
a priest, and on behalf of many who ask you to keep
faith with that sense of calling . . . I long for you to
allow me to minister the grace of God through priesthood. In the mercy of Christ and for the sake of our
Church I ask you: please test my vocation.*

(The Reverend June Osborne, speaking to the
General Synod, 11 November 1992)

On 11 November 1992, the General Synod of the Church of
England voted to ordain women to its priesthood. When the
result was announced, people wept, sang and even danced in
the street in a very un-Anglican display of emotion. The day-
long debate had been broadcast on radio and television, and
the result made the front page in most national newspapers.
THE CHURCH SAYS YES T0 VICARS IN KNICKERS!
screamed the *Sun* next morning, with obvious delight.

This book was commissioned to mark and celebrate that
decision. The first women priests will soon be getting on
with the job many of them have been waiting for years to
do. For some time now they have been performing all the
administrative, pastoral and teaching functions of the clergy
while having to call in a male priest to celebrate the
Eucharist that is the heart of the Church's life. This decision
means that they can now round the circle both in their own
lives and work and in those of their church communities.

The 'yes' vote has been a cause of celebration for all

kinds of people who have worked long and hard for this change, and we welcome this chance to salute their efforts. For all 'interested parties' – both pro and anti the decision – the Synod debate became a focus of the wider debate about women's place in Christianity which has, of course, been on the Church's agenda since its earliest beginnings. So we will start by addressing ourselves to a set of general questions that people ask about the Church.

Why has the priesthood been a male preserve for nearly two thousand years? Isn't this just like the resistance women have met in entering other professions? Surely people will accept women priests, like women doctors and bus drivers, when they get used to them? Or is there some 'special' source of opposition deriving from what Jesus himself said and did – choosing only men for his disciples, for example? Or from St Paul and his odd ideas about women wearing hats and keeping silent in the churches? The people who are threatening to 'leave the church' rather than share it with women priests seem to imply that this decision is some kind of betrayal of essential Christian principles. Why?

Alongside these questions is another set of questions which have been posed by the women's movement, both in the Church and in society as a whole. Will this change really do anything to reverse Christianity's historic anti-woman bias? Can the symbolic elevation of a few – possibly 'token' – women really make things better for the rest of us? Won't it just tempt churchmen to think that now they have set their own house in order they can stop thinking about other forms of sexist discrimination?

Behind this second set of questions lies the spectre of those many uncounted and disregarded women who have left the Church, too wounded by its sexism to stomach its God any more. While the Church laments those who feel that they are forced to leave over the issue of women priests, it has never displayed the same kind of sorrow over those women who have been driven away by the lack of them. Will the long-awaited advent of women priests help to heal these wounds?

It would take a whole book, if not a whole shelf of books, to address any one of these questions in the fullness it deserves. The book we have chosen to write has been directed and shaped by our own interests and experience, so the best way to introduce it might be to say something about ourselves, the authors.

We are both members of the Anglican Church, which means that this is an insiders' book, not an academic overview of religious sexism. There is a place for such analysis – social anthropologists, for example, have done useful and important work on the primitive fears and taboos that have undoubtedly underlain the debate – but this is not that place. As part of the Church we do not wish to distance ourselves from its all-too-human flaws.

We have supported this motion as feminist Christians, which means that the second set of questions is also very much our own. We have been particularly touched by the support of many of our non-religious feminist friends who see this as a symbolic victory for all women, and it is chiefly for them that we are writing this book – to explain how we got here and why we believe that the decision is indeed something all women can celebrate.

This is not to say that we have approached these matters in precisely the same way, or reached the same conclusions about them. Indeed, part of the pleasure of writing this book has been in discovering our disagreements and trying to persuade each other. We have not always succeeded, but it has been interesting to look at why we disagree. We have found that our different ages, personal and professional circumstances all come into play.

Jane came to feminism through a formal study of theology. Theology means simply 'God-talk', discourse about the existence and nature of the Divine – something we all do, but Jane has done it in a more systematic way. It was, however, her own faith in a God who values each person, irrespective of race, class, gender or status, that led her into the struggle to show the Church how far and how often it falls from God's own generous vision of humanity.

Susan, on the other hand, came to theology through feminism. An active campaigner for this cause during the 1970s, she – unlike Jane, who was immured in school and college – was actually present at many of the events outlined in Part II. The 'no' vote of 1978 was a particularly devastating blow for both of us. We were faced with three choices: one was to accept the decision – and hence some of the ideas about women's place which had, on that occasion, been evoked in its defence; the second was to follow a large number of our contemporaries out of the Church. The third, the only real option for us, was to stay in and fight on. But if resistance to women priests was to be overcome, we had to meet it on its own – that is, theological – terms, *and* to connect our understanding to a feminism we had also experienced as a 'means of grace and hope of glory' (as the Prayer Book puts it).

Jane soon realised that the theology she was learning could not sustain its claim to 'objectivity'. While it became clear to us both that what was often really at work in this particular debate was not theology at all but prejudice and custom, Susan found that she could not properly expose the non-theological 'hidden agenda' without a firmer grasp on the official one: the Church's understanding of sex, power, priesthood and ecclesiology (what the Church is).

We hope that this book will reflect the collaboration between formally trained and self-taught theologians which has been an important feature of the campaign, and of Christian feminism at its best. Those disagreements that remain unresolved derive as much from our differing personal experiences of the Church as from theological conviction.

Jane has a number of close friends, some of them Church of England priests whose ministry has nurtured her for years, who have worked, prayed and written with her on issues of race and class, but part company with her on the issue of women priests. Their sorrow and sense of displacement are an inevitable part of what the November decision meant to her, and this concern is expressed in the closing pages of Part III. It does not have the same significance for Susan, who has been nurtured by a different group of people, including her Roman Catholic friends and colleagues who are longing for this and other changes within their own Church. She recognises, however, that it is precisely opponents' very real sense of alienation that the Church of England is currently trying to heal. Not only have its attempts to do so received the lion's share of media attention over the last eighteen months (as readers who have followed the aftermath of the Synod debate are doubtless aware), they will directly affect the conditions under which the present generation of women receive and practise their priesthood.

Virago's invitation to write this book is one sign of how important the Church's decision was felt to be for women *as a whole*. If it is to continue to have that kind of symbolic importance outside the Church, we hope non-Christian feminists will 'keep faith' in their own way with the vocation of June Osborne and others, and will join us in calling the Church to account – go on seeing the victory as theirs, too, so that the Church continues to be answerable, in part, to them, and does not rest upon the supposedly feminist laurels it might be tempted to claim and we might be tempted to grant it.

Susan Dowell
Jane Williams
1994

PART ONE

◆

The Motion Debated

From 1978 to 1992
The Theological Background

IN THE FIFTEEN years since the Church of England last debated the ordination of women and voted against it, the climate has changed in all kinds of ways. Both those in favour and those against spent the intervening years preparing themselves politically and theologically for last November's vote. But if that has its drawbacks in terms of the size of the opposition to women priests, it also has its advantages in that there has been a dramatically increased awareness of what the underlying theological issues actually are.

Laypeople on both sides of the debate have been prepared to plunge recklessly into theological literature of the most technical and abstruse kind in order to make up their own minds on this all-absorbing question. Feminists, in particular, have worked hard to rediscover and re-imagine a more inclusive and women-affirming theology. Women's studies groups all over the country examined the New Testament to discover the traces of a more equal community in existence immediately after Jesus's ascension, before the Church became institutionalised. They delved into the Church's long history to find out what women have actually been doing through all the long Christian centuries, and they discovered that the answer was far more varied than might be imagined from a reading of male historians, ancient or modern.

It rapidly appeared that there were, in fact, large numbers of role models for women in the Church. It has even been argued that there have been women priests in the past. The evidence is a little dubious – based on, for example, some paintings in the catacombs in Rome that may show a female figure with arms outstretched in a priestly gesture over the bread and wine. While it is not clear either that the figure is female or that what is going on is a Eucharist, what is striking is how succeeding generations of commentators and copyists have ignored the ambiguity of many of the figures round the table, have referred to them as 'priests' and even added beards, quite unconscious of how their basic assumptions were showing.

Perhaps more convincing is the ban on women priests issued at the Council of Laodicea in the fourth century. Why bother to ban them if there weren't any? And if the matter could be debated then, surely that gives us licence to debate it now? Even if women priests were the exception rather than the rule, or functioned only in groups judged to be heretical, the point is that the Church's tradition is not as monochrome on this issue as it has sometimes appeared.

Of course, not all role models for aspiring women priests in the Church of England have to come from the past. Denominations like the Methodists, the Baptists and the United Reform churches have long had women ministers, and within the worldwide Anglican Church, too, there were already considerable numbers of women priests by the early 1980s. The sight of them processing down the aisle of Canterbury Cathedral at the great celebration of women's ministries in 1986 was one of the great shifts in consciousness for a lot of people, who until then had seen the issue as one that concerned only the Church of England. Many of these women priests from abroad told their stories. One, from an isolated, snowbound part of Canada, remembers showing her Sunday school children a book about other Anglican children, with pictures of priests from all over the world. One of the children remarked, in shocked tones, 'But that priest is a *man*!'. Those children had experienced only the priestly ministry of women, and the idea of male priests seemed as strange to them as the idea of women priests seems to some of us.

A number of overseas women priests came on extended visits to offer their experience to the ordination movement in Britain. Some celebrated 'illegal' Eucharists; some preferred to respect the Church of England's discipline concerning women priests, and did not exercise their priestly ministry. Some even lived in Britain for years, acting as laypeople or, at most, deacons, even though male colleagues from their countries could act as priests.[1] Partly as a result of the attempt to work with the letter of the law about women priests while breaking the spirit of it, women's liturgy groups began to meet up and down the country, exploring new, more women-affirming ways of worshipping. Hymns, prayers and whole liturgies that began in experimental groups were taken up by mainstream parish congregations.

However, if interest in and knowledge of the changing status of women grew between 1978 and 1992, so did opposition to these changes. Opponents of the ordination of women, too, worked hard at the theological justification for their position, and produced literature for both trained and untrained readerships. The groups that emerged on this side of the debate tended to be specifically campaigning organisations; we will look at them in Part III. But naturally, part of any good campaign is information, and both sides bombarded members of General Synod with literature to prove their point. Both sides also worked vigorously to get their members elected to Synod, since the measure was one that required a two-thirds majority in all three Houses of Synod – Bishops, Clergy and Laity.

Those opposed to the ordination of women were extremely effective in this respect. Although opinion polls had long suggested that laypeople in general were largely in favour, enough lay opponents had been elected to Synod to create a real cliffhanger on the day of the vote. Some of the difficulties that the Church of England is now facing arise from the fact that no one could be sure which side would win in November.

But if one thing emerged more clearly than any other from the years of debate between 1978 and 1992, it was that while both sides were basing their arguments on essentially the same data, their interpretations were wholly and irreconcilably different. Underlying the question about whether or not women can be priests are two other fundamental sets of questions. One is to do with the nature of the Church of England itself: by what authority does it make decisions? What kind of a church is it, and what is its priesthood, anyway? Why has its self-perception made it harder for the Church of England to ordain women than for some other churches? The other set of questions is to do with the nature of women and men: what are the differences between them, and what theological significance do they carry? It is not only in Church circles that these matters cause problems, but the ordination debate made them part of the evidence for or against women priests, rather than just a matter of continuing discussion. In that sense, the uncertainties that run through the whole of society about how women and men should relate have been opened up as never before by the Church's debate.

The theological exposition that follows expresses our certainty that the Church of England was actually right when it said in 1975 that 'there are no theological objections to the ordination of women'. But it is important, too, to understand that those opposed to the ordination of women were not, with a few exceptions, simply the misogynists they often appear to be. The line of argument that leads to a conservative view of the position of women in the Church has long antecedents, even if, as we believe, it is ultimately sterile.

Authority in the Church of England

As June Osborne said in her Synod speech, 'The Scriptures and the tradition are precious to me – they are my guiding stars in the constellation which is Christ – but they are not enough to test my vocation; the Church itself in its life and in its law must validate that call.'[2] This holds true for all branches of the worldwide Anglican communion, but in some Anglican churches the testing was done more gladly than in others. In Canada, for example, there was such a desperate shortage of priests that the ordination of women seemed like a godsend rather than a trial. Ted Scott, Archbishop of Canada at the time, took swift authoritative action to legalise the position of women who were priests in all but name. In America, the situation was different again. Early 'illegal' ordinations were followed by a decision to accept women priests, but the issue was as hotly debated as it is here, and women priests are still not fully acceptable throughout the country.[3]

But although the Anglican Church in America could not force *acceptance* of women's ministry, it could at least make the decision entirely through its own legislative structures. The Church of England, on the other hand, has two specific hurdles to cross before it can make any major decisions – one that is unique to its status as an 'established Church', and one that it shares, to a greater or lesser degree, with all Anglican churches.

Being an 'established Church' means that the Church 'belongs', in all kinds of senses, to people who are not actually practising Christians. In the first place, Parliament has to approve all major Church legislation, which is why women could not be ordained priests as soon as Synod had voted in favour of it in November 1992. Theoretically, Parliament could have declined to ratify Synod's decision, in which case there would have been no women priests in the Church of England, even if all its members had been converted to the cause overnight.

It is also 'owned' by the nation, in the sense that it does not have the power to administer its own funds independently. Church buildings and Church money do not 'belong' to the Church of England to dispose of as it wills; they are administered by the Church Commissioners, who have a legal obligation to ensure that the Church uses its money in ways that are seen as commercially responsible. The decision that was made in November 1992 that priests leaving the Church of England over the ordination of women should receive financial compensation was not a decision that the Church could ratify without reference to its state-appointed 'bankers'.

And, of course, the Church of England 'belongs' to the nation in the sense that non-Anglican – and, indeed, non-Christian – citizens of the state still feel that the Church is, in some vestigial sense, a repository of the nation's values. Church leaders enjoy a remarkably privileged access to media attention, and their pronouncements on matters like, for example, the economy or nuclear deterrence are hotly debated by governments, even though they can no longer directly affect government policy. Many politicians like to feel that they act for 'a Christian society', so they are made to feel distinctly uncomfortable when the Church withholds its blessing.

The same process can be observed with this present issue. When the Tory MP and former member of General Synod Anne Widdecombe announced her departure to Rome after the vote in favour of women priests, she chose to have the ceremony admitting her to her new Church in that monument to the established Church, the House of Commons chapel. This was obviously both a device for getting maximum attention and a gesture symbolising that the Synod decision was, in her eyes, concerned with a betrayal of our island's history.[4] Even though most of the nation will not be affected, in their day-to-day lives, by the presence of women priests in the Church of England, both those who, like Anne Widdecombe, opposed the measure and those who supported it saw it as a blessing of women's changing role and status in society.

But of course, there are those within the Church of England and elsewhere who feel that that is part of the problem. This is a decision based on cultural considerations, not an intrinsically *Christian* decision. As we shall see in Part II, debates about the place of women in the Church have had to be conducted with the wider question of the place of women in society as a whole in mind since at least the nineteenth century. The Suffrage movement profoundly affected Church attitudes and legislation concerning women, although it also prompted some churchmen to call upon Christian women to turn away from the example of their secular suffragette sisters.[5] But by the 1920s and 1930s, the anomaly of a society that allowed women full voting rights living beside a Church that still treated them like children was evident to all.

The record of November's debate shows that the ground has shifted somewhat over the last half-century – though perhaps less than we might sometimes think. One speaker reminded Synod that some of the arguments being used against women priests were exactly the same as those used against women Readers in the 1950s.[6] But at least this time nobody was openly challenging women's inclusion in other areas of the Church's ministry, or their presence in the various decision-making bodies of the Church. The recurring themes this time were: is this a *church* decision, and if so, should the Church of England take it alone? Canon Christopher Colven said, 'We as Christ's witnesses must not be afraid to stand over and above contemporary wisdom, for we are called not to conform to the secular agenda and expectation but to challenge its presuppositions.'[7] He expressed with great clarity the fear of many that day that the Church was being bounced – possibly against its will, and certainly too fast – into following society's view of women, rather than the Christian one.

The Christian view on the place of women in the Church

is one, many people argued, that the Church of England cannot possibly know by itself. As the Reverend Peter Geldard said, 'We are but a provincial synod of two very small parts of Christendom which collectively make up possibly 0.5 per cent of the whole of Christendom.'[8]

This is where the second hurdle facing the Church of England's decision-making processes comes in. The Church of England has generally claimed to take its authority from 'Scripture, tradition and reason'. 'Scripture' is, of course, the records of the Old and New Testaments. 'Tradition' means what the Church has done in the past, and many Anglicans would assume that history has a great deal of weight in helping the modern Church to decide things. In particular, most Anglicans would appeal to the first few Christian centuries as 'authoritative', too, though without the overriding force of the Bible. In these early centuries, which are often called the 'patristic' period, the Church did a great deal of thinking about the implications of the coming of Jesus, and it was in these centuries that most of the central beliefs of Christianity were given worked-out expression – beliefs like the divinity and humanity of Christ, the doctrine of the Trinity, and so on.

'Reason', the third source of authority for Christian decision-making, is the appropriation of Scripture and tradition for everyday living, and their interpretation in the light of God's continuing presence and revelation. Christians and the Christian God are not supposed to be just fossils, forever stuck in the past, or even parrots, only repeating, without thought, what has been said before.

None of this makes life easy for the Church, since there are not very many instances where Scripture, tradition and reason are all clearly either for or against an action, so that the possibility of different interpretations of the same material is always there.[9] In trying to decide whether or not the Church of England should ordain women, arguments from all these three areas came into play, as we shall see in the sections that follow.

The authority of Scripture and the ordination of women

Both sides of this debate, of course, claimed to have Scripture on their side. The Archbishop of Canterbury spoke of 'the same dynamic' at work in bringing non-Jews into the Church in the first century and in bringing women into the priesthood in the twentieth, while Mrs Sara Low spoke of 'the clear teaching on headship' in the letters of St Paul.[10]

Given this confusing ambiguity of usage, it is worth making one or two very obvious points before we go on to look at the different arguments in detail. First, the Bible is not, of course, one book. It is a large number of different books, produced at different times, over a period of centuries, and by very different people. Since all the very first Christians were Jews, their religious horizons, like those of Jesus himself, were formed by the Jewish Scriptures, which Christians now call 'the Old Testament'. All the writers of the New Testament take for granted a certain world-view, shaped by, for example, the Genesis creation stories, the prophets' witness to God's involvement with the world, and the whole story of the Jewish people's relationship with their God over the centuries. This is not one coherent narrative – there are different kinds of communities and concerns at work behind the Old Testament books, and these books are then further adapted and reinterpreted by the Christian writers of the New Testament for their own ends. So you cannot say 'the Bible says' in the way that you could of a work written at one time by one author with one sustained purpose. Instead, you have to weigh up and interpret different strands. There are those within the Church who argue that this is not the case, and that you can, in fact, say 'the Bible says' and settle the issue. But even the most extreme of these – sometimes called 'fundamentalists' – do, we shall argue, interpret the Bible rather than just obey any clearly stated aim when it comes to the place of women.

All the biblical writers take for granted the assumptions of any ancient society about women as 'possessions', viewed only in relation to men. Most would also assent to the Old Testament's ritualised taboo about blood, which means that women are seen as 'unclean' while they are menstruating.[11] Perhaps more vitally, they also take it for granted that the God of Israel and of Jesus is not a sexual being. In the early history of Israel's fight for nationhood, Israel's God is distinguished from the gods of other tribes partly by this very fact: God is alone, without a spouse or family. His creativity, unlike that of other creator gods, is not a *sexual* creativity. He is, of course, still spoken of in predominantly male terms, but this is supposed to denote the fact that God is personal and relational, rather than that he is male. For most practical purposes, in the heavily patriarchal societies in which Judaism and Christianity flourished, this theoretical assertion about how God transcends sexuality is forgotten, and certainly, when the habit of referring to God with masculine pronouns is taken together with the other beliefs about the nature of women and men that we shall explore later, the implications become more sinister. But the genderlessness of God remains one of the basic tenets of all the early Christian writers.

If we turn directly to the New Testament, there are at least two potentially conflicting strands of thought about the position of women. The first is the 'headship' strand, referred to by Sara Low above; the second is what Rosemary Radford Ruether calls 'the prophetic-liberating' strand.[12]

In 1 Corinthians 11: 3, St Paul says that 'man is the head of woman', and although he is often credited with inventing sexism within the Church, here, in fact, he is just expressing a commonly held view, based largely on the assumed structure of creation. In the story of the creation of the world in the Book of Genesis, God makes Adam and Eve. He makes them in a particular relation of hierarchy to each other and to the world. The man is 'the head' of the woman, as human beings are 'the head' of the rest of creation. This hierarchy is obviously intended to be benevolent and nurturing, and when Paul refers to it in his letters, it is always to urge husbands and wives to be caring towards each other.[13] At the same time, however, it is assumed to be a hierarchy that is both natural and God-given, and therefore not one of the things that Christians need to question.

This picture of the tender, if slightly patronising, care of the male for the female is given a more sinister twist, however, when the story of the Fall is taken into account. Eve is particularly blamed for having fallen for the serpent's line, eating the apple herself and sharing it with Adam. So now the headship of men over women becomes not just a natural thing, but also a moral one: the headship of a morally superior being over a morally inferior one.[14] This aspect is seldom referred to in modern debate on headship, but we shall see that it had considerable influence on previous generations' views of women and men.

Paul and the other New Testament writers take the subordination of women to men for granted, but he also assumes that in the Christian community relationships are altered by that central relationship of all Christians to Christ.[15] He expresses this very memorably in Galatians 3: 28, in a phrase much quoted throughout the Synod debate: 'There is neither Jew nor Greek, there is neither slave nor free, there is neither male nor female; for you are all one in Christ Jesus.'

Now, as a matter of fact, these distinctions between people, Christian or otherwise, *do* remain, and the early Christian communities built up codes of conduct on the basis of them, just as all societies have. But it is very hard to know for certain what women could and could not do in New Testament communities. On the one hand, Paul commends a worker from another church, a woman named Phoebe, to the church in Rome, saying 'she has been a helper of many and of myself as well' (Romans 16: 1); and in 1 Corinthians 11: 5, a notoriously difficult passage, he says that women should have their heads covered when (not if) they pray and prophesy in church. Yet 1 Timothy – a letter written in the tradition of Paul, but probably not by Paul himself – says: 'I permit no woman to teach or to have authority over men; she is to keep silent' (2: 12).

None of these passages says anything about whether or not women can be priests. Actually, the New Testament says nothing about Christian priests at all, of either sex. Christ is called High Priest (in, for example, Hebrews 5: 10), and all Christians are called a royal priesthood (see 1 Peter 2: 9), but it is not clear that anyone is actually *ordained* in the New Testament. The various forms of ministry being exercised by people in the New Testament churches cannot be mapped directly on to our present-day priesthood.

So the point is that in order to formulate a 'biblical' case either for or against the ordination of women, an argument has to be *constructed*. One set of texts – either the ones about a new standard of relationships among Christians, or the ones about the subordination of women – has to be *chosen*, and the other minimised. This is not a new difficulty. On other issues, too, theologians have had to use biblical texts to answer questions that the biblical writers did not pose. The obvious example is that of slavery. New Testament writers take it for granted that there are slaves, and they give advice about how Christians should behave towards each other, whether slave or free. Not until the nineteenth century did the Church come to realise that equality in the sight of God is not consonant with a state of affairs where one human being can own another. Biblical exegesis was often said to uphold slavery, simply because the biblical writers never thought to condemn it; but a deeper examination of the radical claims of the Gospel made it clear to nineteenth-century reformers that slavery must be abolished.

Those who would argue against women's ordination on the grounds of male 'headship' are, in fact, being rather more obviously inconsistent than those who argued in favour of slavery on biblical grounds. In the biblical context, 'headship' is not primarily about priesthood, but about the order of creation in general and the marriage relationship in particular. No one who took 'headship' literally could accept the Queen's governorship of the Church of England, or Margaret Thatcher's premiership, or any other exercise of female authority. Within the Church, they should also object to women preaching and teaching – both activities which the New Testament sees as 'authoritative'. In other words, they have already so sold the pass on the 'headship' issue as actually found in the New Testament that it is strange to object on those grounds on an issue which the New Testament does not even mention – the priesthood one.

So, in practice, the decision about which New Testament line on women is the one for us to follow has to be made in conjunction with an understanding of the Church and its priesthood – what are they for, what have they been in the past? In other words, Scripture has to be read in the light of 'tradition'.

Tradition, reason and the ministry of the Church

Although, as we saw above, there may have been women priests in certain isolated places and times in the Church's past, clearly the Christian priesthood has been overwhelmingly male for most of its history. In that sense, the ordination of women is something new. As Alec Graham, the Bishop of Newcastle said in the Synod's debate: 'Whether this is a legitimate development of the tradition . . . is either "not proven" or a straight "no".' But of course, churches do have to do things that have not been done before, and the Church of England owes its very existence to a willingness to take new action at the time of the Reformation. As another speaker in the Synod debate, Dr Paul Avis, put it: 'Then it was affirmed that a branch of the Catholic church had the right and duty to reform itself, including its ministry.'[16]

So the question is one about the primary duty of the Church: is it there *essentially* to be faithful to the witness of the past, or is it there *essentially* to bear witness to God's presence now? Should it fear and distrust 'secular' trends as liable to corrupt the sacred treasure of the past, or should it see God continuing to work through his creation now as he has in the past?

When the question is framed like that, most Church people would have to answer that the Church must, unfortunately, do both those things, and the Church of England is in a peculiarly difficult position in that it claims to be 'catholic' while it is no longer 'Roman Catholic'. It was born not just out of the compulsive dynastic urges of Henry VIII but also out of a dissatisfaction with the way in which the Church was then being run. Any reader of Chaucer will know the kind of rackets that most laypeople assumed most priests were running – Church corruption was one of the standard themes of comedy. So the Reformed Church in England claimed to be returning to purer, more original roots – to be, in fact, the true 'catholic' Church, leaving the 'corrupt' papal Church as a kind of degenerate rump.

The Church of England – unlike some of the other Reformed churches, such as the Lutherans or Calvinists – made no sweeping changes in the structure of its ministry. But like other 'Protestant' churches, it did make a significant theological change in its understanding of priesthood. In the pre-Reformation Church, some priests were ordained simply and solely to celebrate the Eucharist, with no kind of pastoral duties attached at all: they were there simply to offer 'the sacrifice'. Protestant Reformers particularly objected to this use of the word 'sacrifice' in connection with the Eucharist, since it smacked of pre-Christian religion and since they also insisted that the only sacrifice necessary had already been made by Christ on the cross. Many Reformed churches deliberately avoided using the word 'priest' of their functionaries, since 'priests' were those whose duty it had always been to 'sacrifice'.

The Church of England continued to speak of 'priests', but it did reject the Roman identification of the priestly duty as primarily a sacramental one. Instead, it put much more emphasis on the caring, shepherding duties of the priest, and in this respect it had much more in common with the Reformed churches than with the Roman Catholic church for most of the period from the Reformation to the nineteenth-century Tractarian movement. But it did not make any fundamental changes in the way in which authority was exercised within the Church. Some Reformed churches chose to make the local congregation the central authority, but the Church of England merely transferred papal authority to the king, and a complex theology of the 'divine right of kings' to rule held sway for a considerable length of time. When this theology waned, the Church of England was left with no very obvious decision-making channels. It had neither the papal authority nor the Protestant freedom to reform, and while General Synod is acknowledged to have *legislative* authority, it does not carry the theological weight to enforce its laws. Both sides in November's debate implied that they would defy Synod's decision if it went against them.

There is, then, a real uncertainty in the Church of England about how to exercise contemporary 'reason' on a 'tradition' that is shared with other churches. The Reforming churches that chose deliberately to start a new, uncorrupted line of ministry, based directly on their understanding of New Testament ministries, do not have the same problems about making further changes in ministerial structures: they are bound to 'tradition' in a very different way. For them, the shifts in understanding brought about by modern scientific and biblical discoveries – as outlined below in Part II – were grounds enough to admit women to the ministry. They did not have the added weight of a shared 'priesthood' to worry about.

Nowadays, of course, 'priests' and 'ministers' have far more in common than they did in the immediately post-Reformation churches. Ministers in all churches would expect to have pastoral and sacramental functions, though which of the two carried the most weight would vary from denomination to denomination, or even congregation to congregation, since 'High' and 'Low' Church groups in the Church of England would not always offer the same description of ministerial functions. But those churches that still think of their 'priesthood' in heavily sacramental terms have experienced particular problems in relation to the ordination of women, as we shall see.

The revival of this way of understanding the priesthood within the Church of England, together with the resulting uncertainty about its right to take autonomous decisions, has its theological roots in the Oxford Movement of the nineteenth century, which also largely shaped our contemporary understanding of the structure of the Church and the nature of its priesthood. Since it is precisely on these questions of Church and priesthood that the issue of the ordination of women bites, it is important to see how those words are being used.

The nature of the Church and its priesthood

The Oxford Movement of the 1850s is often cited by the 'catholic' wing of the Church of England as the foundation of modern Anglicanism. In fact this movement was a continuation of a religious revival that spanned the century and took a variety of forms.[17]

The leaders of the Oxford Movement consciously tried to

recover a number of lost pre-Reformation elements for the Church of England. In particular, they emphasised the Church of England's claim to 'catholicity', and they did this partly through a theology of the priesthood. For them, the priesthood came to focus very particularly in the *sacramental* activity of the priest at the Eucharist. This is the thing that sets the Church apart from the state, and gives it its supernatural authority.

When this is allied with a strong belief in apostolic continuity, it makes the priesthood even more theologically vital. The Oxford Movement's main writers, like Edward Pusey and John Henry Newman, argued that the Church of England, through its priests, can trace a line right back to the earliest New Testament Church, and even to Jesus. Just as Jesus commissioned his apostles, and they, in turn, commissioned their successors, so the process goes on throughout the generations, with each generation ordaining the next generation in unbroken line. When a bishop lays his hands upon the head of a newly ordained person, he is doing what has been done since the Church began, and he is sharing with the new priest an office that has been passed down in this way from the very earliest days.

So bishops and priests have a very particular responsibility to the history that they have symbolically shared in through their ordination. They have to be aware not only of their own individual ministries but of the ministry of the whole Church, throughout the world and throughout all ages.

Although there were, of course, good and faithful ministers in much of the post-Reformation Church, they carried out their duties without any greatly elevated view of the 'priesthood'. If you read the novels of Jane Austen, or the diary of Parson Woodforde, it is clear that the eighteenth-century Church was just one more profession among several for the gentry. Parson Woodforde was doubtless a decent sort of man, but he does not seem to regard his calling as a 'vocation'. In most churches at the time there would seldom be a Communion service, the clergy would hardly bother to dress up, and many church chancels were used to store old furniture.

It was the early-nineteenth-century Evangelical movement that began the revitalisation of the Church of England. Its leaders did much to bring a new moral vigour to Christian faith and practice: the campaign to abolish slavery, for example, was spearheaded by William Wilberforce, a devout Evangelical. Wilberforce's clergy colleagues and followers were men of impressive piety, dedicated to their parishioners and full of zeal for reforming the Church, but their energies were not directed towards a recovery of the theology or language of priesthood.

The revaluing of the priesthood as a sacramental calling, then, was a particular, distinctive contribution of the Oxford Movement. Although the Oxford Movement was viewed with suspicion as 'Romanising', and Newman himself eventually became a Roman Catholic, its legacy is a vision of the Church of England as 'catholic', as part of the universal Church, claiming a direct line of succession from the apostles.

As we saw above, modern biblical and historical scholarship has made this theory untenable in its simplistic form – Jesus probably ordained no one – but the fact remains that within a hundred years or so of Jesus's death, the Church was generally using the words we now use to describe ministers: 'bishops, priests and deacons'. So these offices have existed in the Church for nearly two thousand years, even if their function has varied slightly from age to age. And for the whole of that period they have been filled, almost without exception, by men.

When it is put like this, the case against the ordination of women has obvious strength. Women priests might well be a dangerous novelty – not because they lack piety, or the ability to 'do the job', but simply because they break the line of unity with historical tradition. But this argument can make it sound as though the priesthood is simply a matter of being as old-fashioned as possible. What is it that the ministry of the Church is actually supposed to do, and would it really be so torn from its historical roots if women did it?

Most theologies of the priesthood assume that the priest's relationship to God is no different from that of any other Christian. All Christians, through their baptism, share in Christ's life and join in his saving work of bringing the world nearer to God. The Church appoints particular people – 'priests' – to remind it, constantly, of its calling. They remind it of its original calling, from Jesus, by their ordination in a historic line of descent, as we saw above. Through their preaching, teaching and celebrating the sacraments, they constantly connect the historical element in all those acts with the Church's present task and the future towards which it is looking. So the priest's relationship to the Church is that of exemplar. That does not mean that priests have to be better behaved than the rest of us, but that they remind us of our common calling.

Priests do this symbolic work largely for the local community they serve, while bishops connect the local church to the universal Church. Bishops are supposed to represent the local church to the world Church and the world Church to the local church, reminding the local church of the tradition which makes it and reminding the universal Church of the worshipping communities that actually give it flesh. This is why the bishop is sometimes called 'the focus of unity', and there are very particular theological problems for a definition of the Church when bishops cannot do this representative job. If what the bishop has to bring from the local church to the universal Church is a priesthood that is exercised locally but not acceptable universally, then the focus is broken. This is the case with the ordination of women, and has been so since the first Anglican Church ordained a woman priest.[18]

We shall see in Part III what implications this has in

practice, but in this context it is enough to emphasise two things. First of all, this point about unity is, in our opinion, the most theologically serious one of all the points raised by those opposed to the ordination of women. Secondly, it is *not* a theological difficulty created by the Church of England's decision in November 1992. It is one that the worldwide Anglican Church has lived with and worked with for nearly twenty years. Although we do not deny that this is a serious question mark against the ordination of women, it is so only if it is admitted that allowing women to be priests and bishops *changes* those orders in some vital sense, rather than just making slight local variations in them, as is permitted in all churches.[19]

Opponents of the ordination of women have attempted to demonstrate that maleness is theologically essential to priesthood, not just a historical accident. In its contemporary forms, this is in fact a radically new theological argument – obviously, since the question was not seriously raised in previous centuries. St Thomas Aquinas debated the matter of whether women were capable of priesthood entirely theoretically; he did not expect his reasoning to have any practical outcome. But do theologies of the essential maleness of the priesthood hold water?

They are based upon the idea that the priest – and the bishop, in particular – stands as an 'icon' (image, or picture) of Christ to the Church.[20] In particular, as the priest offers the 'sacrifice' at the Eucharist, he re-enacts the sacrifice of Christ. So this is now given as a reason why the *Eucharist*, in particular, should not be celebrated by a woman. As the priest celebrates the Eucharist, he symbolises the self-giving of Christ to the world. What is vividly re-presented at the altar is the action of the historical Jesus: first in sharing the Last Supper with the disciples, then in sharing himself with the world, through the crucifixion.

The symbolism becomes particularly concentrated when it is the bishop celebrating the Eucharist, focusing local, universal and historical churches while presiding at a sacrament that symbolises the local, universal and historical presence of Jesus in the Church. The bishop is the one who 'passes on' the priesthood, through ordination, from generation to generation, and he is the one whose office, through its links back through history, is to guarantee the continuity and orthodoxy of the Church. So when he stands at the altar, celebrating the Eucharist, he is symbolic of the 'body of Christ' in a very particular way – the historical Christ, and the people of Christ throughout all ages, who make up his 'body', the Church.

Opponents of the ordination of women have argued that a woman cannot stand as the icon of Christ in this way. A woman breaks the threads of connection with the historical Jesus, who was undoubtedly male. The argument is that the particularly dense and satisfying sacramental framework is shattered by changing the sex of the priest. 'And because the ordained priest is not exercising a priesthood of his own but is the agent and instrument through which Christ is exercising *his* priesthood, he too must be male,' E. L. Mascall argues.[21]

But no one has ever argued that the Eucharist is a kind of play. Priests are not chosen for their likeness to first-century Palestinian Jews. If the priest does not have to look or sound like Jesus – and how could he, since we don't know what Jesus was like – in any other way, why is his *maleness* non-negotiable? As the Archbishop of Canterbury reminded Synod during November's debate,[22] the first-generation Church assumed that all Christians must be Jews, since Jesus was a Jew and preached primarily to Jews. The earliest Christians had to be shown that the Gospel was not bound by rules of culture. Perhaps our generation is learning that it is not bound by rules of gender, either.

The danger is that if maleness is made the *only* non-negotiable tie with the historical Jesus, it has to be given such heavy symbolic weight to explain why this one characteristic cannot be changed that the argument often seems to imply that Christianity is not a religion for women at all.

As we said above, traditional Christianity has always claimed that despite its overwhelmingly male language about God, God is neither male nor female. This should be quite obvious, really, since God does not have a body, and therefore cannot be sexual. So male language about God, like all the human descriptions we give to God, is said to be 'analogical' – it tells us something truthful about God, but it is the description offered by an artist's impression rather than a set of measurements.

But – as those who use the 'icon of Christ' argument point out – we do have one non-analogical picture of God, and that is Jesus. And Jesus was certainly a man. But again, traditional Christianity has never made theological use of Jesus's maleness. The central theological point of the incarnation is that God becomes human.

The classical doctrine of Christ is that Christ becomes incarnate – becomes a human being – to save the whole of the human race. So it is essential that he was completely human, not just pretending, so that our human nature is shown to be capable of transfiguration. This has been so central to Christian theology that one of the Church Fathers, Gregory of Nazianzus, argued that if there was any part of our human nature that Jesus did not share, then that part did not share in his saving work ('what was not assumed was not healed').

Absolutely fundamental to this argument is an assumption about common humanity. Obviously, Jesus was a particular person – he could not and did not share in all the experiences that each individual has. But he shared in the common lot of humanity – and that must mean *humanity*, not just manhood, otherwise women are not included in Christ's saving work. In other words, if Christ's *maleness* (rather than his humanity) is central to God's saving purposes, then women are not saved by Christ. Women will have to wait for a female incarnation of God to 'assume' and 'heal' their human nature.

In fact, throughout the history of the Church, the icon of

Christ argument has never before been used to justify the maleness of the priesthood.[23] Of course, most previous generations took it for granted that priests were men, but they did not use the icon of Christ theology to justify this. (Aquinas argued that it is women's inferiority/subordination that makes them unfit to be priests, not Jesus's maleness.)

If some opponents have argued that the priest must be male, then others have argued that the priest must not be female. C. S. Lewis made the point that a 'priestess' is something quite different from a 'priest'.[24] Priestesses did exist in pagan cults contemporary with the beginnings of Christianity, but Christianity rejected them. 'Priestesses' often functioned in nature cults which were concerned with seasonal growth and with fertility, so their biological functions of menstruation, pregnancy and childbirth were part of the symbolic structure of the cult. There is some residual belief that women priests would automatically become *sexual* symbols in Christianity in a way that male priests apparently are not.[25] It is as though women can function, symbolically, only in their biological aspect, whereas male action can function symbolically in other fields as well.

But if 'maleness' is not part of the essential symbol-structure for being a Christian, why is it essential for being a priest? If women as well as men can be baptised, then they are already part of God's new life, already 'in Christ', representing and being represented by him. If it does not make sense – as it really does not – to say that only men can 'act' Christ at the Eucharist, then some other criteria must be operating in the assumption that priests must be male. There must be an already assumed theology of maleness. No theory of priesthood – whether that of the 'icon of Christ', or Lewis's 'priest/priestess' distinction – can function on its own as a reason not to ordain women. Proof has to be offered on other grounds that maleness is an *essential* characteristic of God's action in becoming incarnate. Only if it is believed that God *had* to become incarnate in a man, because only maleness carries the right symbolic message, can the icon of Christ argument function as a reason not to ordain women. As we shall see in the next section, some opponents of the ordination of women do argue precisely that.

In summary, however, the vital point being made in this section is that arguments that rely on 'maleness' as theologically vital to a definition of priesthood seem to be being used in very novel ways nowadays by the opponents of women's ordination. And if the theology that justifies excluding women is as lacking in traditional basis as is the decision to admit women to the priesthood, then the opponents of the ordination of women must admit that they are in exactly the same position as those in favour. We are all involved in appropriating Scripture and tradition by means of reason. Neither outcome has a privileged relationship to the tradition, unless it can be shown that men and women are, *theologically speaking*, entirely different creatures. Definitions of the priesthood do not, in themselves, seem to require maleness unless there is already some previously held understanding of what women and men are before God that makes female priesthood such a profound change that no one Church is able to implement it alone.

So what exactly does Christianity have to say about women?

'Male and female created he them': women and men before God

How did Christian theology get into its present peculiarly uncomfortable position about sex (the missionary position, perhaps)? As we have already said, God is traditionally spoken of as beyond gender, yet God's activity, on which priestly activity is to be modelled, is sometimes said to be more 'like' male activity than female activity. This strangely illogical position is based upon largely unspoken assumptions about the proper relationship between male and female. But if we examine 'the Christian position' on male/female stereotypes, it turns out not to be so clear-cut and divinely inspired as some opponents of the ordination of women would imply.

As we saw in the previous section, the biblical evidence on this question points in two different directions: the subordination of women is taken for granted, but so is their participation in the 'new creation' through Christ. Of course, the biblical position is not formed only on internal Jewish-Christian assumptions. New Testament and early Christian writers were also influenced by the Graeco-Roman culture in which they lived, just as modern Christian assumptions about the proper relationship between women and men are also a strange amalgam of attitudes from the distant and not-so-distant past, and more recent research on the subject.

This complex web of assumptions was hardly ever spelled out in the period of debate before the Synod decision, but we believe it is absolutely fundamental to the question of whether or not women can be priests. As we saw in the previous section, many arguments that purport to explain why all priests must be male cannot in fact do so without being able to show what 'maleness' is, and what it means theologically.

Previous generations seem to have had quite definite ideas about what 'male' and 'female' are; systems of philosophy and theology have reinforced these and, in turn, been strengthened by them. Classical biology, for example, assumed that women were defective men. If everything goes according to plan in the womb, then what emerges is a male child. But if something goes wrong, if the temperature in the womb is too low, then the child is not 'baked' hard enough; it comes out softer, colder, less defined – a girl, in fact. So, from birth onwards, men are rational, active, full of the vital force of life; while women are irrational, prone to fits of rage, and unreliable. This was thought to be biological fact – medical researchers of the period thought that their researches confirmed this state of affairs.

If this 'biology' is set against the kind of philosophical assumptions that you can see, for example, in Plato's work, some interesting things emerge. Classical philosophy assumes that what is real is unchanging and rational. It was thought that men being more rational and less changeable than women, were more 'real', more like the Divine – their activity more nearly mirroring the divine reality, and their government of society more likely to approach the divine government of the world.[26] What emerges, then, is a dualism which has far-reaching social and philosophical effects, but is based upon supposed biological fact. Without its 'factual' grounding, this philosophy would not be convincing – though equally, of course, the philosophical assumptions helped to shape the biological 'facts' uncovered; on the whole, people found what they expected to find when they performed biological experiments.

The writers of the New Testament and patristic periods would have shared the assumptions outlined above. Christian feminist scholars have often pointed out the misogyny and dualism of much patristic writing, as though this was a Christian invention rather than a set of culturally conditioned assumptions, shared by all writers of the period. Christian scholars may have justified their view of women partly on 'scriptural' grounds (for example, the story of Adam and Eve), but their conclusions were remarkably similar to those of non-Christian ancient writers.

It is striking that, given this web of justification for the subordination of women, Christian writers still acknowledged that women could have spiritual status within Christianity. In particular, women who in some way negated their sexuality could be 'honorary males'. They could achieve this either through celibacy or through martyrdom; then their hybrid state – physically women but spiritually men – could be very edifying for the whole Church.[27] The very unlikeliness of such weak and irrational creatures managing to be faithful to God made them more marvellous than their male counterparts.

So, from the beginnings of Christianity, a wild card has been introduced – that women, inferior as they are, are still called by God to be examples and servants for the Church. No Father of the Church, however misogynistic, ever attempted to deny this, although he might see such women as very much the exception rather than the rule. Certainly, the prevailing assumption was that women were subordinate and inferior to men.

It is important to remember that this inferiority is not worked out in psychological terms. There is no Jungian analysis of 'masculine' and 'feminine' archetypes. Instead there is a simple assumption of a status quo, based upon biological research and reinforced by a philosophical system. There is no need even to attempt to justify this state of affairs in terms of the psychological or social skills of women and men. It can just be assumed that this is the way things are.

Christian asceticism added an extra dimension to men's distrust of women. Although the classical world assumed that it was bad for men to indulge in extravagant amounts of sexual activity, for fear of diminishing their vital male heat, it was also taken for granted that all decent responsible citizens would father as many children as they could. The infant mortality rate, for those who managed to survive the birth process itself, was so high that it was, in fact, vital to produce children. But Christianity did not have a vested interest – at least in the early centuries – in continuing society. Christians looked, in fact, for the end of the world, for the breakdown of the pagan Roman world, and the emphasis on sexual restraint as a mark of commitment to the new world was inherent in Christianity from the beginning. With the growth of the monastic movement, this emphasis on celibacy as the 'more perfect way' grew, and with it the literature reviling women as sexual temptresses also grew. Women were the ones who caused men to abandon their exalted discipline, women were in league with the tempter to drag men away from their prayers. The fact that men tempted women away from their spiritual lives was neither here nor there. What grew was the image of women as devilish temptresses.

What were women, then, in the first few Christian centuries? They were irrational, inferior, liable to pull a man down from the heights, but capable, with God's grace, of attaining spiritual stature, despite their unspiritual natures.

But we do not move in that world any more, and we could not even if we wanted to. No one in November's debate put forward the theory that women are inferior and irrational (at least, not in so many words; though some did argue that women are sexual temptresses – we shall look at that in a moment). Instead, those who argued, on the basis of the Bible, that women are not supposed to take leadership roles in the Church had already substantially shifted their grounds from those of the early Christian writers. We can no longer believe the biological and philosophical foundations that the biblical writers took for granted, so the position has to be justified on different grounds.[28] What they then argue is that women are not so much inferior as simply different.

This view has, we believe, two different sets of roots. One is the Victorian romanticisation of women as actually, in many respects, *superior* to men. It is easy to forget what a novel idea this was, and although it worked as another restrictive stereotype in some ways, it also gave some of the great Victorian reforming women their moral justification. Not all women, of course, benefited from this new elevation: it seldom applied to working women, only to the protected women of the middle and upper classes. But these women were supposed to be *more* spiritual than men, though not in an active, outgoing way. Instead, they were to be the quiet enablers and inspirers, the ones who kept the home as a wholesome place of growth, the ones whose sweet, frail loveliness was to inspire their menfolk to go out and conquer and convert the world.

This saccharine vision somewhat undermined the way in which the myth of the 'honorary male' had grown within Christianity. Whereas previously women could really be spiritual equals for men only by denying their sexuality, around the figure of the Virgin Mary a way evolved in which women, *as women*, could be spiritual. This was a way of passive acceptance, of joyful response to male initiative, such as Mary was supposed to have shown in giving birth to Jesus. Through her acceptance of a properly female role, Mary was thought to have redeemed humanity from the curse brought upon it by the forward action of Eve. Mary then becomes a model of how redeemed women should behave.[29] This attitude to women is still very prevalent. One could cite the Pope's advice to the raped Catholic women of Serbia: that in bearing the violence and nurturing the children of violence, they are fulfilling God's will for them, and acting as exemplars for their war-torn country.[30] A woman's role is still supposed to be defined by her female biological functions and by her passivity, and within that role women become exemplary Christians – in theory, at least. In practice, men are usually encouraged to admire this example, but not to emulate it.

In all kinds of ways, the Church has exploited this view of women as – within certain carefully defined limits – actually more spiritual than men. We all take it for granted that there are more women than men in church congregations, but this spirituality becomes instantly invalid, apparently, if it moves beyond the domestic confine, or out of the convent. What is now argued is not so much that women are inferior, and therefore incapable of priesthood, but that certain kinds of spirituality are 'feminine' and not 'masculine'. This position is reinforced by certain kinds of psychology, which form the second set of roots for the modern justification of women's different position in the Church. Like the notion that women are in some sense 'superior' to men, this set suggests that women are wonderful but *different*.

Jung, for example, speaks of the 'masculine' and the 'feminine' as two distinct archetypes, with different qualities. He is clear that each male or female person is actually a mixture of 'feminine' and 'masculine', but his system is often used loosely to justify the stereotyping of qualities between the sexes. So women are said to be instinctual, nurturing, emotion-orientated, while men are rational, creative, action-orientated. The experimental basis for these differences is hotly debated,[31] and it is interesting to see how little the actual qualities have changed since the time of Plato, although the interpretation put upon them has, since the sexes are now said to be 'equal but different', rather than just superior and inferior.

What happens in theological terms is that women can now be spoken of glowingly, while they are still denied all access to power. Women have a proper place in the Church, one that can be described in dauntingly honorific terms: 'The vocation of every woman is to protect the world and men like a mother, as the new Eve, and to protect and purify life as the Virgin. Women must reconvert men to their essential function, which is priesthood.'[32] The description is still entirely in biological metaphors – virgin and mother – and it is quite hard to define exactly what it is that women are supposed to be *doing*. This wonderful protecting and reconverting role is actually suspiciously vacuous.

Women, then, are still seen in largely passive terms, and their 'receptivity' is then used as a reason why they cannot be priests. Priesthood – the performance of sacraments – is a creative, penetrative act, not an accepting, nurturing act, so the argument goes; it must therefore be performed by men.[33] This strange mixed metaphor is obviously heavily dependent upon a male view of the sexual act. It is also surprisingly like the classical biological view of women as merely containers for the active male seed. Yet such metaphors now have force only if the imaginative description of 'masculine' and 'feminine' is accepted. There is no longer the 'assured' biological foundation for this kind of philosophical speculation that writers of earlier centuries could assume.

The Church of England's debate in the run-up to November's decision showed, we believe, a horrible confusion about the place of women in our society and in the Church. This confusion reflected the history at which we have been looking.

Much of the opposition to women priests was based upon an assumption that priesthood is 'inappropriate' for women, because priesthood expresses God's outgoing, creative, dynamic aspect, and all those characteristics are assumed to be male. We have seen how such a view of maleness worked within a particular biological and philosophical framework, but how does it work now? Every bit of that assumption can be challenged – from its definition of male and female activity, to its definition of priesthood, to its definition, finally, of God. For although most arguments against women exercising ministerial authority have historically rested upon perceptions of *women's* essential nature, not God's, arguments that stress the similarity between male activity and God's activity come perilously close to an odd, if not heretical, description of God as a male person.

Some opponents, like the retired Bishop of London, Graham Leonard, reflected the view of women as sexually dangerous. He said in a radio interview that if he saw a woman in the sanctuary, he would be unbearably tempted to embrace her. Now this view is not, of course, limited to Christianity. Islam shrouds women from head to toe because the sight of too much female skin is dangerously exciting to men. The interesting thing about Leonard's statement is that he did not find it at all odd that only women in the sanctuary become so wildly erotic. Most congregations are made up largely of women, and most male clergy seem to resist their charms (though you might not think so if you read the tabloids). So is it actually just powerful women who so excite the bishop? The other thing that is never acknowledged is that women, too, might find priestliness sexy. Several of Barbara Pym's novels are based upon the fact that women fall in love with their vicars, and this is thought funny and just a little bit sad, but it does not function as a reason not to ordain men.

It is not only opponents of the ordination of women, however, who emphasise the sexual overtones that women will bring to the priesthood. Many supporters of the ordination of women also seem to suggest that we need women priests because we need 'womanliness' in the priesthood, and this 'womanliness' is often equated with experiences like childbirth, with images drawn from the fact that women's lives are dominated by a monthly cycle. In other words they, too, treat women as primarily *biological*.

Yet none of these experiences is common to all women, and if we emphasise them we are in danger of playing into the hands of our opponents. We are trying to say that women have something special, unique, to offer Christianity – something that has never been properly heard before, since Christianity has hitherto really listened only to the male experience of life. The danger is that the opposition also say that women have something special and unique to offer Christianity – something that has never been properly heard before. But they argue that to ordain women is to try to cram this 'specialness' into a male-shaped container – the priesthood – and that this allows male experience to dominate once again. What is needed, they suggest, is a better attempt to find a real, feminine ministry for women in the Church, rather than forcing women to emulate male priestly ministry.

So both sides of the Church's debate have used the argument that women are 'equal but different'. We have tried to show that this is not a biblical position at all, nor would it be recognised by most patristic writers. Instead it is a grafting of Victorian Romanticism and post-Freudian psychology on to a biblical base. The Bible and the Church Fathers assumed that women are inferior to men, and that any equality they gain is an equality of grace, rather than nature. Later thinking assumed that, within their limited sphere, women could be spiritually superior to men, but that their finely drawn natures would be damaged by contact with too much harsh reality. A confused mixture of these two views lies, unacknowledged, behind a lot of November's debate.

We have tried to show that some attempts to prevent women from becoming priests originated not in ill will but in thorny problems of theology and ecclesiology. But the blame also lies in a profound and very real uncertainty about how to describe the relationships between men and women. This difficulty is not confined to Christianity. Feminist debate is still polarised by the question of whether women should be given equality because they are basically the same as men, or because they are basically different from men. Is our demand for equality based on the assumption that our skills are the same, and so cannot be denied, or different, and so necessary?

But surely the point is that this is the wrong question. So long as we are still making our decisions purely on the basis of gender, we are failing to see the wood for the trees. In ordaining people to the priesthood, there should be no talk of anyone's 'natural' fittingness, since the whole thing is a matter of God's grace. Nobody is born a priest; priests are made by a mixture of God's calling and human need. Far too much of the debate has centred upon the respective positions of 'women' and 'men' rather than the gifts of individuals, and whether the Church has need of their particular skills in the priesthood.

History also reveals that generalisations lead to positions that are clearly dubious. While some of the Church Fathers were writing vitriolic treatises on women in general, they could, almost at the same moment, be writing deeply moving tributes to their wives.[34] For every statement you make about 'women', you can find almost as many exceptions as confirmations.

So much of this debate has been conducted without really returning to first principles. The first principles are that much of our Scripture and tradition understands the relative positions of women and men in terms of a biology and philosophy that *no one can accept any more*. Even so, both Scripture and tradition recognise that God's grace can take women out of their 'proper', 'natural' places, and give them equality with men. So when we no longer have an assured 'natural' basis for saying what women can and cannot do, how secure do the arguments against God's grace look? The Church's failure to ordain women in the past is based on certainties we cannot share. The only way to test our own beliefs is to try it and see what happens.

This is not a dangerous break with the past. We have been trying to argue in this part that the Church's view of the place of women has always been culturally conditioned, just as its view of the function and place of the priesthood has been dictated in part by cultural assumptions. In trying to respond to our changing culture, we are not doing anything intrinsically unfaithful. We are not abandoning the historic threefold ministry of bishops, priests and deacons, simply deciding that in our culture, women may enter it. The General Synod is not the Pope. It makes no claim to infallibility. It makes the best decisions it can, based on Scripture, tradition and reason, as to what the Church should do. It does not and cannot say: 'All Anglicans must believe this', but merely 'This is what we are going to do'. The rest is up to God.

In Part II we look at some of the hopes and fears that supporters of women's ordination brought to the Synod debate last November. What has kept women in the Church, for all its sexism? What did they have to do to get the Church to the point of actually having to decide upon this matter? And has the price of 'victory' been too high, either in personal terms or in terms of a larger commitment to the feminist issues of justice and equality?

PART TWO

◆

Those In Favour . . .

To CONSIDER SOME of these questions, we now turn to some stories of women who have sought priesthood for themselves. We look to them not to provide the answers to these and other questions we raise in this book, but, rather to acknowledge that they have lived and struggled with them in a very particular way. Laywomen like ourselves may well feel diminished by the barriers, both theological and social, that the Church imposes on women, but they do not affect us as directly as they affect those women who offer their whole lives to the Church as priests. So what brought – and keeps – these women here, at what now, clearly is the sharp end of the whole debate about women's place in the Church?

They stay, of course, for the same reason we all stay and the role lay supporters like ourselves can most usefully play in this struggle is a crucial question to which we will come later – because we love the faith, and although the Church continues to madden women it also nourishes them, as it has throughout its long patriarchal history.

Women have always played the 'wild card' of their equal belovedness of God (if not of men) for all its worth. At the same time as it has led them to heroic acts of obedience to the Church, it has also led them to resist the manifold limitations inflicted upon them by this male-ordered institution over the centuries. Although, as feminist theologians and historians have now established, this resistance has been going on in some form or another since Christianity's earliest beginnings, it was not until the late nineteenth century that sustained arguments for women's admission to the ministries of the mainstream denominations were advanced.

Feminism and Church in the nineteenth century

Why then? Why not before? To answer this question we need to look more closely at the conditions under which women played their strange hand throughout the nineteenth century. Assumptions about women's 'natural' subordination began to be seriously and systematically questioned. In no other period, as Kate Millett writes, 'had the question of sexual politics or of women's experience within it grown so vexing and insistent as it did in this'.[1] Even had it wished to, the Church was unable to stay out of the fray, for the theological, ethical and social consensus on which all its teaching and practices were based was also being challenged more rigorously than at any other time in Christian history.

The erroneous biological basis of these assumptions has already been mentioned, but it was only one of a series of misapprehensions which were cleared away by the steady advance of science. Darwin's theory of evolution and modern biblical scholarship were both made possible by the development of fields of study – archaeological, linguistic and anthropological – which were inaccessible in earlier periods (much of the background information on biblical texts in Part I was unknown until the nineteenth century).[2] Darwinism and biblical criticism combined to undermine belief in the literal truth of the biblical account of human origins; and as 'Man' himself came to be seen as an evolving creature, shaped by environmental and social conditions, it became easier to see 'his' relationships in the same terms. This also applies to the relationship to the Creator – and we now know that what was once considered bedrock biblical teachings, like the notion of 'one God', was a fairly late

– 40 –

development. Engels's version of 'the beginning', published in 1870, took these investigations still further by examining 'early man's' relations with his female partner. His suggestion that patriarchy might not have been the first form of human society was to become fundamental to feminists' deconstruction of patriarchy in general and patriarchal religion in particular.

Many people, of course, were entirely untouched by these revelations, but they stirred a current of unease in a Church whose political and intellectual dominance had been seriously undermined by the Enlightenment.

The accelerating effects of the Industrial Revolution had an immediate impact on the lives of both sexes. The appalling conditions of the new urban underclass made it impossible for thoughtful Christians to believe in the God-given/'natural' order of society, and many came to see that they had a Christian duty to involve themselves in the political arena. Such public activity was not thought appropriate for women: indeed, the new romanticised view of women presupposed their equally novel situation of confinement to the domestic sphere, set apart as never before from the world of production. It was from the sacred hearth, far removed from the real world men inhabited, that women were expected to guard the souls of these same men, and the moral values of their nation.

But women, too, found that the works of mercy expected of Christians – and now of Christian women above all – could no longer be conducted on a purely domestic or neighbourly basis. Middle-class women began to take up a whole series of causes – temperance, Abolition, the plight of their 'fallen' sisters, and the position of sweated workers: The prodigious influence of Christian women's groups was noted as early as 1842, and because the public welfare projects they set up were entirely women-initiated and women-run, those involved had to acquire a range of administrative and communication skills that women had simply not needed hitherto. Most important, perhaps, was the confidence they gained in women's ability to work together.

So long as women had real channels through which they could exercise their ministry, the question of ordination was not felt to be an urgent one. This is not to say that no individual woman at this – or indeed, any other – time felt herself called to be a priest. St Thérèse of Lisieux (d. 1897) actually spoke of her longing for priesthood, and saw the onset of her terminal illness as God's kindness in taking her before she was old enough (twenty-four) to become a priest, 'in order that I may regret nothing'.[3]

But such vocations were never joined to, or even appear to endorse, a women's ordination *movement*.

Origins of the ordination debate

By the end of the nineteenth century, however, the openings and opportunities women had taken up with such enthusiasm began to be closed off to them. The home and overseas missions they had pioneered and staffed expanded rapidly, and were 'taken over' by the mainstream churches and brought under a predominantly male central authority.[4] Women found that they needed some kind of formal status themselves if they were to keep their stake in these fields.

The other option, of course, was to work – as many, including devout Christians like Florence Nightingale, did – outside Church structures. More and more women began to take paid work, sometimes of necessity, sometimes – and mightily inspired by the Suffrage movement – from a need for independence. The First World War pushed women even more fully into public life, and increased professional opportunities for women meant that servants became unavailable to all but the very rich. The slaughter in the trenches left countless women without husbands, and therefore any opportunity to 'work from home' for the benefit of the wider community; this further shrank the pool of middle-class female volunteers.

The churches responded to these changed conditions by opening up a number of positions, with proper pay and training, in which women could work as missionaries, youth workers, parish assistants and administrators. Soon denominations which had no substantial theological problem with admitting women to their ministerial structures began to do so (though the Lutherans and the Methodists did not take this step until the early 1970s) and the numbers of ordained women began to rise steadily between the two world wars. The Anglican Order of Deaconesses, created in 1862, was enthusiastically taken up by increasing numbers of women in the first half of the twentieth century. We should also mention the foundation, also in the 1860s, of the Anglican Sisterhoods. Nuns can be – and have been – used against women who wish to be ordained. For much of the Church's history, enclosed sisterhood provided the only forum in which women could serve the Church, and the bias against sexual womanhood ensured that they were seen as the highest model of true Christian womanhood. But this was not so within nineteenth-century Anglicanism: so strong was the 'angel-in-the-house' myth that many clerics and laypeople denounced the Sisterhoods and their founders on the grounds that they prevented women from fulfilling their sacred duties as wives and mothers. It can be claimed, then, that the new nuns, along with other 'professional' women, provided an important counterbalance to the idea that a home-based ministry was the best, or the only, way for women to serve God and the community.[5]

First and second waves of Christian feminism

The 'professional' Christian woman had arrived. There can be no doubt that she has contributed immeasurably to the well-being of the people and communities she served, and to the Christian community as a whole: the twentieth century is rich in examples of brilliant and creative women ministers. But when we turn to the question of their influence upon the position of women – both in their own denominations and in the Christian community as a whole – we cannot claim any dramatic improvement.

Part of the problem lies in the fact that we are talking about women who were in every sense 'exceptional'. The Protestant denominations did not make any concerted move towards ordaining or licensing women ministers: they acted according to particular circumstances as these became pressing, and women were admitted one by one, on the basis of pastoral need or personal merit, rather than as a matter of social or theological principle. Although this is entirely consonant with Protestant theology of ministry, it has tended to prevent these professionals being seen – and seeing themselves – as representatives of ordinary lay Christian womanhood. This was something over which the women themselves had no control; they were trained either alone or in twos and threes, in institutions set up for and run by men. Everything about these places, from the language to the lavatories, must have confirmed these women's sense that they were honorary members of a male club, there entirely on merit.

On the other hand, the visible presence of ordained women in some denominations, combined with increasingly widespread support for the Suffrage movement, had a significant influence on those individuals and denominations who did not think it necessary or right to take the step of ordaining women. The Church League for Women's Suffrage was founded (in 1909, reaching a membership of five thousand by 1914) both to secure the vote and to draw out 'the deep religious significance of the women's movement'.

Although there was still no single-issue pressure group for ordination (the League itself was divided on the question), there were strong reasons to suppose that the Church of England would soon take this step. The Deaconess Order was widely regarded as a precursor to full priesthood (all male priests are 'deaconed' before ordination, which almost automatically follows a year later), and not until 1935 did the Church officially declare that deaconesses were authorised Church workers and, as such, members of the laity rather than in 'holy orders' like their male counterparts. Elsie Baker, a veteran of the present campaign, was ordained before 1935, so – as she insistently reminds all concerned – she has been in holy orders for well over fifty years, ordained to a broken promise.

Maude Royden (1876–1956) is the best-known casualty of Anglican ambivalence towards women during this period. Born into a rich Liverpool family, Maude, like so many other women of her time and class, fought her way out of the drawing-room to do welfare work in the slums. Her astonishing skill as a public speaker was developed in her work as a university extension lecturer promoting peace and suffrage issues. Urged by a clergyman friend, she began to use this gift in his London church, and soon became a star preacher with a huge following. The Bishop of London, although he was a strong supporter of women's suffrage, became alarmed and forbade her to speak or preach in Anglican Church buildings. Royden was torn between her followers and the authorities and accepted a preaching job at the City Temple, a large Nonconformist chapel. She has been an inspiration to countless women who have heard or read her sermons, and we can rejoice that her gift was not lost to the wider Christian community. At the same time, because her own story is such a sad one – she died hurt and embittered by her own Church's rejection of her gifts – she stands as an example of women's need and right to claim their vocations within their own chosen Church communities.

Anglican women did not give up on their particular struggle, but by 1930, with the vote secured and first-wave feminism beginning to die down, the ordination movement stalled – and, as has so often happened with feminist endeavours before and since, divided. Two groups came out of the old League: one, the Anglican Group for the Ordination of Women, continued to press the specific question of ordination; the other, the Society for the Equal Ministry of Men and Women in the Church, was concerned with the more general 'depreciation of women's work and total ignoring of their status in the church'.

A good deal of thinking went into both questions, and in 1948 the World Council of Churches published a comprehensive analysis of discrimination against women in twentieth-century Christianity.[6] But these explorations were now being conducted by 'professional' theologians in the higher echelons of ecclesiastical bureaucracy – like the World Council – and they did not, by and large, filter down to the ordinary 'woman in the pew'. What she saw and heard in her church in the 1950s and 1960s was male clergy in charge of predominantly female congregations who were in many cases expected to do no more than raise money and make countless Victoria sponges. Churchgoing women whose consciousness of discrimination had been sharpened by 'second-wave' feminism had no obvious way of changing this situation – and certainly no organised protest movement to join.

Bread or a stone?: 1970–90

By the late 1960s, things had begun to change. More and more women became frustrated and began to ask questions. Because these questions were not being answered by the Church, women turned to one another, and small Christian feminist cells began to spring up around the country.

It was the Christian Parity Group (CPG), founded by Dr and Deaconess – and now Sister – Una Kroll, which provided a vital bridge between the younger constituency of Christian feminists and the older groups mentioned above. Along with Elsie Baker, who had a strong guiding hand,

Una had long felt called to be a priest herself, and both women were well placed to affirm and nurture the increasing numbers of younger women in the same position. The 1975 decision (that 'there were no theological objections' to women's ordination) had once again produced a general air of expectancy. Would the Church at last produce the new deal for women demanded, as more and more of us came to believe, by its Gospel?

Many will remember Una Kroll's cry from the public gallery of Church House when the 'no' vote was announced in 1978: 'We asked for bread and you gave us a stone.' (Why the second part of her cry – 'Long live God' – has been excised from the records, even by those of her most ardent supporters, remains a mystery.) The most poignant memory for those of us who were present was Una comforting a young woman whose hopes and plans had just been dashed; as she wept bitterly on Una's shoulder, a gentleman of the press congratulated them both on a touching 'performance'. It has been hard to forgive him, particularly as some of us knew that Una had already laid aside her own vocation. Fighting for other women from such an exposed position – Una had been subjected to relentless ridicule from the press and derision and anger from the clergy throughout the whole lead-up to the debate – effectively precluded her from being accepted as a 'suitable' priest herself. In a recollection of the events leading up to 1978, 'never before asked for or spoken', Una has written:

I knew about not being eligible for priesthood just before Alison Cheek [a US Episcopalian priest, ordained illegally in 1974] came to celebrate the eucharist in the Unitarian Church in Golders Green in 1976. The invitation had been extended in CPG's name by two of our members . . . during my absence overseas. I had to decide in conscience whether or not *I* could go along with it. It was a difficult decision for me as I had felt it was politically dodgy at that point, 'inexpedient' as they would say. So I could have disassociated myself from it, and many of my church going friends were, at that time, writing and telling me to disassociate myself from 'those people', i.e. feminists, lesbians and gays, lest 'I harm the cause of ordination and set it back by 50 years!' So I wrestled those few days with what I really did believe and want for myself. And I can recall the moment of decision vividly, because it was made, in the end, in a flash while I was looking out of a window at some beautiful trees. I *knew* that to buy into respectability for the sake of being an acceptable person to the ecclesiastical authorities was, for me, a betrayal of all I believed or said I believed at that time. If women like myself were to abandon the outcast, the militant feminists, the unacceptable people for whom Jesus died, we would be betraying Christ and buying ordination at their expense. And so I backed the venture, abandoned respectability, and knew what I was doing. It was not without cost, for I remember weeping at the pain of bereavement from 'my own' vocation for a couple of days after that before I could return to be fully committed to the visit and the work involved in helping the 1975 Sex Discrimination Act get under way.

The reason behind my 'leaving' visible leadership for total commitment to prayer, beginning in 1979, when I left London, [was] that I do not believe in *one* woman leading and knew that unless many women led and led differently (as they have done) we would never get anywhere.[7]

We have quoted this letter in full because it is, for both of us, a deeply moving reminder of the questions and tensions Christian feminists were struggling with then – and still are. What is the relationship between feminism and Christianity, and how should it be expressed? Are women priests buying into the system at the expense of the wider feminist struggle? How 'respectable' should the movement be? What do we hope for – and from – women priests?

First, however, let us set the context in which these questions are debated today.

The wider, more collective leadership Una Kroll saw to be necessary was established in 1979 with the founding of MOW (the Movement for the Ordination of Women). Like CPG, MOW set out to function both as a 'supporters' club' and as a forum for the wider theological debate, and it has made enormous progress in both areas. Its successful programme of raising public awareness has ensured the earlier-than-hoped-for reintroduction of this matter before Synod. It has also managed, far more successfully than could reasonably have been expected, to gather together under one umbrella the moderates to whom Una Kroll referred in her letter and the more upfront feminists who, along with Una herself, had consciously identified themselves as dissidents, and found their true home in the informal structures of Christian feminism.

MOW is not – and does not pretend to be – 'the voice of Christian feminism'. The informal cells continue to flourish: Christian feminists still meet to pray, sing, study and tell stories. New groups have sprung up. Some, like WIT (Women in Theology) and the St Hilda Community, are daughter movements within the ordination campaign. WIT, founded in 1983, aims 'to advance the theological education of women and make available, to women and men, theological insights'. Thus it works to build bridges between the institution and its more radical critics, and to train all sorts of women, lay and ordained, for whatever new models of ministry may emerge in the future Church. Unlike WIT, which exists in cell groups all over the country, the St Hilda Community is a fixed 'church' based in a particular place – East London – with a particular 'congregation'. It was founded in 1987 – partly to worship in inclusive-language forms, partly to experience women's priestly ministry. St Hilda's was one of the groups which invited ordained women from overseas to celebrate the Eucharist; at one time it had its own 'parish' priest, the Reverend Suzanne Fageol.

Another important development in this period was the increasing availability of background material on the subject of women's ordination. Volumes of feminist theology – mainly from the USA, where the movement had long been established and funded – became more widely available, and by the early 1980s British women had begun to publish their own reflections on faith and feminism.[8] A rapid progression from pamphleteering on the ordination question to full-length, commercially published, nationally reviewed volumes setting out the wider Christian feminist agenda has had far-reaching effects. It has substantially added to the store of literature available to the many clerics and laypeople who were moved to explore this question for themselves, and led to a greater openness to women's needs and perspectives among people generally. Even more important, perhaps, is the effect on Christian women themselves: many have said that they have come back to or decided not to leave the Church because feminist theology has made Christianity available to them again. Women's exclusion from the means and sources of theological reflection has proved as dispiriting as our exclusion from the Church's ministerial structures.

Moreover, it is within Christian feminism – in both its rapidly developing theology and its informal structures – rather than in the institutional Church that many women have developed their vocations to priesthood: the movement gave them love and shelter and encouragement to go on, as is borne out in the testimonies of Liz Canham and Kath Burn, two British women who were ordained in the USA.

Liz Canham's Church background was one which many readers will recognise, and some will have experienced: 'To compensate for the turmoil of adolescence I adopted a belief system which provided security by its dogmatic assertions, one of which focussed on the subordinate role of women.' Even when she began to recognise her vocation, it was hard to resist the Church's claim to wisdom and authority in these matters. Having been taught that her Church's rejection of her gifts 'was divinely inspired', Liz Canham felt 'compelled to suppress any desire for leadership in the church and to deny a part of myself without which I felt incomplete'.[9] She did not break free from this stance until a more radical approach to Scripture and a more structural analysis of political questions led her to see the parallels between her own marginalisation and that of other oppressed groups.

Kath Burn, on the other hand, is a 'High Church' Anglican who, from childhood, 'loved the church people and . . . the splendour of colourful worship. I found a relationship with God in Christ and was glad of the sacraments to help make it real for me.'[10] Subordination was not enjoined upon Kath as it was upon Liz (the particular biblical injunction that women keep 'silence in the churches' does not carry as much weight in her Church tradition or, as Kath herself suggests, in the kind of working-class community she grew up in). Both women felt destined to give their whole life to the Church, and set about doing so within the vocations their own tradition most warmly affirmed. Liz taught; Kath trained to be a missionary, and spent three years 'in the field' teaching in Pakistan. Later she joined the Little Sisters of Jesus, a Roman Catholic community in Dublin, in order to test her own vocation as a nun. But for both women it was only when their feminist consciousness had been raised to a certain point that they could see sexism, not themselves, as 'the problem'. As Burn puts it:

Church experiences since confirmation were beginning to fit into place, as the significant pieces of a jigsaw puzzle are suddenly easy to slot together when you see a glimpse of the whole picture. The realisation that I was a *woman* in the Church, with all the implications of that, had sharply come into focus.[11]

She records that it was during her convent time – when she met an ancient and very particular form of sisterhood – that she felt fully accepted as the person she was:

> I affirmed much of their community life. I had talked a great deal with [the sisters] about the vocation of women as priests, *and they had not been horrified by that. They just knew it wasn't their particular calling, but they seemed open to the possibility of it being a calling for other women.* [emphasis added][12]

So, of course, was the Christian feminist community she found on her return to England. Kath records her sheer relief at unburdening herself to Una Kroll, who introduced her to the Christian Parity Group, where she found the support she needed for the next stage of her journey.

Kath and Liz were both accepted for training and ordination in the USA, where they found parish jobs. This became an interim solution for many other women who simply wanted to get on with their work as best they could. They may have had to leave home in the sense of becoming emigrants, but a broad base of support for their calling spared them the pain of exile from their Church roots that had been imposed upon women like Royden.

A feminist issue?

But MOW, as the official voice of the movement, had to give space to widely differing experiences and ideas. For some MOW members this was definitely 'not a feminist issue'. For others, like the present writers, it clearly was and is, now as in the past. The sisterhood that was now being proclaimed in the wider women's movement was, we saw, something that Christian women had lived out in useful and interesting ways over the centuries. Our understanding of recent history suggests that women priests should never be allowed to forget their debt to the whole feminist struggle.

However, they have not been helped by feminists, inside and outside the churches, who seemed equally anxious to deny that this has anything to do with feminism. This is just one manifestation of the somewhat troubled relationship between Christianity and feminism which has become the subject of intense and sometimes acrimonious debate over the last twenty years or so.

Part of the problem lies in the real difficulties we all have in connecting our feminist experience to that of the past. In pre-Enlightenment times, of course, there was no feminist movement as such, and in so far as most people were assumed or compelled to be Christian, it makes even less sense to speak of a consciously 'Christian feminism'. Feminism owes its primary origins to an Enlightenment which, among its other benefits, removed the obligation to be Christian. One could do the kind of 'good works' described above with no reference to God or hope of heavenly reward. This was fully recognised by our nineteenth-century feminist foremothers, Christian and non-Christian alike. The social reformer Harriet Martineau, for example, was an avowed atheist. The endeavours of women like Josephine Butler, Octavia Hill and others, on the other hand, were directly inspired by Gospel imperatives. But notwithstanding (or perhaps because of) passionate debate between the two groups, nineteenth-century Christian feminists clearly respected, were respected by and worked alongside their non-Christian sisters in ways we have either failed to emulate or been prevented from emulating.

A vastly different relationship exists between secular and Christian feminism today; this must be faced up to by those of us who wish to lay any sort of claim to the social or symbolic importance of this campaign. The present-day proportion of Christians to non-Christians, both within society and within the women's community, is an important factor, but not the only one. The British Women's Liberation Movement of the early 1970s arose from and within the Left. The Marxist concept of religion as the opiate of the masses, combined with a harsher-than-ever feminist analysis of patriarchal religion, has led to deep divisions between secular and religious feminists. This was far more markedly true in Britain than in America, where many more people go to church and even the most radically minded do not consider it an odd or unprogressive pursuit. Rosemary Ruether, a prominent US theologian, remembers having extreme difficulty convincing a BBC radio interviewer that there was *not*

> an irreconcilable conflict between 'secular feminism' and the church and it took a good while to bring [the interviewer]' round to seeing the lines are not drawn that way here [i.e. in the US]. It is more like a conflict between feminism and anti-feminism within and between different wings of the church and of society as a whole.[13]

Because feminists in America were not automatically identified as leftie dissidents and/or 'enemies of the faith', it was far easier for the liberal press, and the liberal establishment generally, to see and support ordination as part of a progressive/liberal package.

The fact that Christian women in Britain found themselves standing within the 'enemy camp' of patriarchal religion in a more sharply defined way has had a profound effect on their self-awareness, and on the way the whole debate has been perceived and conducted in this country. It led some women ordinands to feel – and to stress publicly – a distance from 'women's libbers', and to a period of introspection, even timidity, among the most ardent Christian feminists. Looking back at Christian feminist exchanges during the 1970s, it is remarkable how many women said they operated as closet feminists in the Church and closet Christians in the women's movement – which suggests that neither side really wanted to know about the other: the Church was busy dismissing feminism as incompatible with – or irrelevant to – good Christian womanhood; the women's movement was seriously doubting whether Christians could be feminists at all!

Some pro-ordinationists wished to express the feminist connection in the boldest possible terms. One of the ways they did so was to engage in 'direct action' in support of women priests. In the first and most notorious public protest, a small group (including Susan) disrupted an ordination service at St Paul's Cathedral in July 1980 by standing up with banners during the liturgy in order to draw attention to women's exclusion. Other Christian feminist groups have chosen more discreet forms of protest. As noted above, some, like the St Hilda Community, have quietly subverted the Church's rules by taking part in 'illegal' Eucharists which have provided direct experience of women's priestly ministry combined with more participatory non-sexist ways of worshipping.

These two forms of resistance have provoked quite different but equally interesting reactions. The second has met with considerable paranoia – what were these women *doing*? – and legal action to prevent activists using Anglican Church buildings (although attempts to stamp out such groups have been ineffective, since other churches have gladly opened their doors for such occasions). The first caused a public furore, both at the time when the group were frogmarched, quite violently, out of the building, and later, when they were dubbed harridans and harpies who had 'spoiled the young men's day' – as if it had been their wedding or some other private family occasion: a promotion to their firm's board of directors, perhaps? The group had in fact chosen its moment with great care, standing up during the creed, the point in the service when Christians stand together and proclaim their common faith. They were showing that this was precisely not a private occasion, it was the day on which a group of Christians were offering themselves as servants to the body of the crucified servant. Was this a time to shield them from the wounds of other members? Some thought not, including the

Archbishop of Canterbury, Robert Runcie, who telephoned Monica Furlong, who led the demonstration, to say that although he did not approve of our action, it had made him realise the depth of women's hurt and anger as nothing else had.

We are not suggesting that the first action was a braver and better form of protest than any other. Important spiritual and theological insights have emerged from 'illegal' services, and from liturgy groups in general, and it is clear that those who take part in them do so not just to make themselves feel better but to nurture new forms of worship and community in which the fullness of God is more abundantly experienced and shown forth to the world. But gatherings of like-minded people are no substitute for proclaiming 'the message' to those who have yet to hear it. As the Suffrage campaign had amply demonstrated – and as our own experiences of addressing the 'unconverted' has also shown us – issues also need to be exposed in the most public, even possibly proclamatory, ways possible. Women did not get the vote solely by pressing their case in a quiet, reasonable manner, or – as some still maintain – through their stalwart labours during World War One, and suffragists were quick to recognise the important contribution of the militant suffragettes.

The 1980s provided some further opportunities to reconnect our own theological perspectives with those of the wider women's movement. Greenham Women's Peace Camp welcomed all women's peace perspectives, and at major actions and open days certain gates around the base were designated as 'religious gates', giving Christian women and women of other faiths a place in which to pray for deliverance from the 'false gods' of war and patriarchy. The Greenham Vigil,[14] a twelve-hour dusk-to-dawn liturgy, was an empowering and moving experience for participants as well as providing a much-needed night watch for the permanent campers. (A confiscated banner from the St Paul's demonstration was retrieved – with considerable difficulty – and pinned, with enormous pride, to the Greenham fence two years later.)

Christian feminism flourished throughout the 1980s. More and more women began to 'do' theology, formally and informally, producing works of a breadth and depth unparalleled in Christian history. Many of these works focused on the connections between women's oppression and those other evils which were daily, hourly, threatening the world with extinction – militarism, nuclear war and ecological destruction. A growing sense that we were all in the same fragile boat together undoubtedly contributed to the healing of some of the divisions between religious and 'secular' feminism. A greater openness to spirituality as a real and important part of women's lives was signalled by the appearance of collections on 'religious' themes on the lists of feminist publishing houses, and the growth of a worldwide compendium of popular fiction specifically concerned with recovering women's spiritual roots.[15]

However, the broadening debate did not always work to the advantage of those who wished to be ordained, or to that of the campaign as a whole. It certainly alarmed our more tentative supporters, who wondered if ordaining women would lead to 'canonising the Greenham women', as one churchman of our acquaintance put it. That in itself was not so dispiriting as the growing impatience among pro-ordination feminists. As we admitted to each other during preparatory conversations for this book, we have sometimes found ourselves bored with the whole thing, impatient at the time and energy it was taking up.

Ordination was increasingly – and quite rightly – perceived as only one of a number of issues we had to work on, but it was hardly the most exciting, or even the most challenging. After 1985, when the Women Deacons measure – an important first step towards the priesthood – was passed, many people saw the battle as already won. It was not, of course, but it was limping forward to some sort of conclusion, and from then on it became more a matter of legal nuts and bolts than a revolutionary new idea.

Garden or wilderness?

Organisations like MOW continued the hearts-and-minds campaign, and to support the women ordinands during the dry and difficult period of waiting.

Although, as we hope we have made clear, we do not believe this measure will of itself solve the problem of sexism, for some people, both inside and outside the Church, ordination is still the be-all and end-all issue facing Christian women. So it remains extremely important to stress that it is not, and that we must all, lay or ordained, continue to insist on altogether broader explorations of women's relationship to Christianity.

But awareness of the danger of overinvesting in institutional change can be expressed in ways which are hurtful to those who are struggling within the institution: it can even tip over into doubts about whether such change is possible, or worth seeking at all.

Some Christian feminists abandoned the campaign altogether and began to seek an authentically woman-centred spirituality, uncontaminated by the forms and dogmas of male religious authority. Taking their model from the Old Testament story of the children of Israel fleeing Egypt, they identified themselves as an Exodus community, a Woman-church in the desert.[16] We are not opposed to women who took this direction – it has led them to discover spiritual resources in themselves, and to encounter past forms of female spirituality which official Church history has scandalously neglected. But like-minded people, even those who are engaged in important and interesting work, can easily overestimate their influence in the wider world. And if insights gained 'on the edge', in the wilderness, are not brought back to the centre, what real transformation can they bring, except to an enlightened few? Monica Furlong, who has given long years to MOW before herself 'moving on' to these other areas, asks whether this quest for 'self-discovery' is not actually 'hampering the changes we claim to want', and believes that it is important

> for both to listen to each other . . . to recognize that MOW's long struggle for women's ordination is not an irrelevance to those much farther on, but a cutting edge which forces innumerable people, who would otherwise never bother to know about their sexism and confront it. And it is important that they support their sisters, struggling with the synod or the media, recognizing the pressures and loneliness of their stance.[17]

Given the many ways in which Christian feminism *has*, despite denial and rejection from both 'sides', been fed by the wider women's movement, we should not be surprised to find these separatist tendencies reinforced by secular feminism as it developed in the 1980s. In her important book *Is the Future Female?: Troubled Thoughts on Contemporary Feminism*, Lynne Segal argues that feminism as a whole gave up on the struggle for equality and parity with men, and opted for a vision which saw a 'large and inevitable gulf between the needs and values of women and men'.[18]

While it was no longer dismissive of religion and spirituality *per se*, the 'new' feminism also appeared to be far more interested in 'inner' experience than in outer forms, and adopted some quasi-religious myths of its own. 'Real' feminists were those who celebrated women's 'otherness', their *'essentially'* nurturing and peace-loving qualities. Women who collaborated with the enemy – men – on any level were viewed with scorn and suspicion, and those who actually sought to enter any bastion of male power were beyond the pale: 'fembots', in Mary Daly's terms: female 'careerists' lacking in true womanly values, betrayers of the womanly culture that would alone save the world.

Christian women ought to have been the first to remind the movement that although notions of women's 'otherness' have been stated in feminist-promotional terms today, their origins lie in an entirely different place. They have functioned longer and more effectively in the form of patriarchal resistance to sharing real – that is, social and institutional – power with women. The Church has been particularly fond of telling us that 'real' – that is, spiritual – authority has always rested with us, and that 'real' women do not need the trappings of priestly power. So there must now be a certain irony in the remembrance that it was precisely this kind of ideology that our foremothers fought so hard to overcome.

This kind of thinking had particularly depressing implications for Christian women seeking entry into the most male-dominated of all institutions, and it certainly contributed to the 'pressures and loneliness' experienced by women ordinands. These have increased rather than decreased with the successful outcome of the campaign. The popular media continue to isolate women priests from those of us who offer a lay perspective: the common format for radio and TV programmes which deal directly with ordination – rather than with the wider agenda of Christian feminism – is a straightforward debate in which the women are lined up in equal numbers against their opponents and asked the same old questions: How can *you* let *your* 'ambitions' cause so much pain and division?

Most women priests, with the help and encouragement of MOW and other supporters, have kept their heads, their humour and a more practical and historically informed feminist perspective. The fact that members of all disparate factions of Christian feminism stood together outside Church House to await and celebrate the results of the Synod vote indicates that few had really forgotten the importance of embodying new visions in institutions, even one as flawed as the Church.

But some doubts and fears must, and do, remain. Past and

recent history has also revealed the Church's long-practised skill in co-opting individual women's talents and energy in ways that do not disrupt or challenge its sexist structures. So it is deeply disturbing to discover, after more than a decade of intensive discussion of this problem, that a number of women deacons do not seem moved to address or overcome it. Some have refused to join MOW because they do not wish to be associated with its 'stridency'.[19] This really is grossly unfair to MOW in particular, and lay supporters in general. We have no objections to women deacons keeping themselves apart from our more 'upfront' campaigns. This has been an absolute necessity in some cases: there are women we cannot name here who hold their present parish jobs on condition that they do not actively campaign for ordination – their own or anyone else's. Even when 'a low profile' is not strategically necessary, it may still be more appropriate for laywomen like ourselves to draw as much of the opposition fire as we can. It is far harder to put the usual labels (ambitious, unwomanly, etc.) on women who want to receive the priestly ministry of their sisters than on those who want to 'do' the ministering.

But we want more from women priests than that there should be priests who are women ('vicars in knickers'?). If God is not more in the image of man than of woman, neither is God more in the image of a priest than of a layperson. That the clergy have historically become – and seen themselves to be – 'set above' the laity is perhaps inevitable, but it is none the less a distortion of both the feminist and the New Testament vision of mutual ministry. Women's exclusion has been a potent sign of this distortion, and we hope that women would have a particular interest in healing the old divide between clergy and people.

So why are there still women who do not seem to have made any kind of connection with the hopes and fears of their feminist supporters? A worrying example of this position appeared in a letter written just after the vote from Westcott House, a theological training college in Cambridge:

> I rather object to being associated with feminists. I think the whole feminist lobby has done much damage to the cause of women in the church; and to interpret women's ordination as a feminist issue is misleading. I believe that women should be considered for priestly orders not because ordination should be considered a 'woman's right' or even on the basis of equality and justice, but because gender is irrelevant in this case.[20]

It is tempting to dismiss this letter as pure anti-feminism. Parts of it are downright offensive: what on earth is this writer – and other non-feminist ordinands – saying to those women who pioneered this struggle? Can any woman priest really believe she would be being ordained today if women before her had not engaged in 'misleading' talk about justice and equality?

But we, too, have argued that 'gender is irrelevant' to the priesthood – like many women priests themselves, such as Eleanor McLaughlin, whose gentle wisdom and scrupulous scholarship have inspired us both for many years. She writes:

> I am not of the persuasion that priests who are women will or should be priests in radically new ways as is the view of those who look to women to dismantle the . . . authority structures of the Church. One is called 'To be with God with the people on your heart' and whatever inner-authority is a priest's by grace and by virtue of office and presidency will now simply be carried by women.[21]

Moreover, it is important to acknowledge the uniqueness of each individual's vocation to priesthood. For us all, there is an irreducible element of 'inner' spirituality: each of us has to spend time alone with God, attending to God's word to the individual soul. In that sense, too, gender really is irrelevant. The private, individual nature of women's call needs, perhaps, to be particularly stressed at a time like the present, when ordination has such a high public profile and might be thought the 'in' thing to seek.

But none of this suggests that we can ignore the corporate dimensions of this question. Priesthood is mediated by the Church on behalf of and within a community, its needs and its changing consciousness. We are all affected by events outside ourselves: for women, lack of expectation has always been as insidious a destroyer of female creativity as lack of opportunity, and there is a constant interflow between the two. The fact that many women are catching the priesthood bug is something for which we and they should not apologise. Since we started work on this book we have met a number of women – including several Roman Catholics – who, having trained in areas their churches authorised, now realise that they wish to serve as priests. They repressed this call when it seemed impossible to answer it – there is no virtue in eating one's heart out for the impossible – but take the changed situation as God's way of pointing them in a new direction. Eleanor McLaughlin gives a touching example of this when she writes that she became a teacher of medieval Church history because it was 'as close as she could get to the altar and ministry' until 'the Church moved'.[22]

So we must still ask: what kind of priesthood can be offered today and in the future by those who seem to be cutting themselves off from women's long history of struggle? This concern has been movingly expressed by Penny Nairne, a veteran of the present campaign:

And what will I do in the future with my vexation at the horrid habits of the clergy? When our vicar is a woman, if she issues irritating orders, I won't be able to shrug them off with the thought that it's so like a man. When my friend has become a priest, will she still be a sister? What difference exactly will it make?

> What IS a priest? I ought to know, but find that I
> don't. Perhaps none of us does fully . . . yet. For the
> garden merges into the beckoning wilderness.[23]

Or does it? As we move on into the future, we have to take
account of inevitable tensions that can arise between the
pioneers and those who come after them. We should be
thanking God that we need no more lone pioneers and, as
women who are fast becoming members of the older
generation ourselves, be on our guard against the kind of
resentment that can be provoked when younger sisters
appear to clear hurdles their forebears have stumbled over.
Still less do we wish to lock the next generation into the
forms and concerns of this generation's feminists; as we
have just indicated, some brands of feminism do not appear
to have much to do with the liberation of women – all
women – at all. But if any one of us, lay or ordained, gives
up on the whole feminist debate about ministry, then gender
will once again become a burden – by the very nature of
things it can never be totally 'irrelevant' – and if that
happens, the generation after this one will have to reinvent
the wheel all over again.

Meanwhile, back on the farm . . .

The present and future generations' ability to sit lightly and
gracefully in their new calling will depend on the resources
and support they find in the official Church, among the
people they serve and among their clerical colleagues. While
it is to be hoped that women priests will blur the line
between clergy and laity, ministers and those ministered to,
there is no doubt that once they are ordained they will be
part of, and work for, 'the system'. Nobody is going to get
a job 'being' a Christian feminist. So in this section we will
be looking at the system itself – the Church, its clergy, and
its place in the world.

We begin with those who provide our present 'models of priesthood'. A useful way of assessing the pressures upon women is to compare their path to priesthood with that taken by men. Men's path has been – to put it mildly – considerably smoother than women's. While men are tempted to fight or flee 'the call' – and they have many good reasons for doing so – it will generally meet with warm encouragement from their worshipping communities. It is an in joke of Anglicanism that a chap who looks as if he is taking his faith very seriously, attending most services and helping the vicar at every opportunity, must be destined to 'go all the way' and get ordained himself – the unmistakable implication being that priesthood is really where it's at. When a woman does this she is thought tiresomely pious or interfering – the 'vicar's scourge', poor man. (Whereas she may now be thought to be harbouring clerical 'ambitions', in past times it was usually thought that what she wanted was to marry, rather than be or help, the vicar. The 'role' of clergy wife is still a commonly suggested 'displacement activity' for churchy-minded women!)

But men, as well as women, have worked to change all this. Earlier in this century, before there were significant or influential numbers of theologically trained women, it was male arguments that most nearly carried the day:

To deny to women the outward and visible sign and acknowledgment of their ministry is not only to be false to the example of St Peter and Cornelius[24] it is to make unreal the whole sacramental ordering of the Church. Where God's gifts are manifest and effective, the failure to authorise them is not merely a wastage but a denial of the true character of Christian organisation.

But there is a further principle involved. The Church, if it is to be the body of Christ, fully representing his fullness of life, cannot do so while it is represented and controlled by one sex alone. There is, in

Jesus, the perfect quality of man and woman alike, the paradox of diastole and systole, of individuality and community, of adventurousness and home-making. The embodiment of the Divine can only be fulfilled in the complete humanity of a man–woman partnership. Until the Church gives true status to both alike it will not reach a fully Christian level of being, it will remain power-ridden, dualistic, unstable.

When at last after aeons a real partnership in secular affairs has become possible, it is a tragedy that the Church, in which as in Christ there should be neither male nor female, allows itself to be enslaved by its own traditions (and by less worthy motives) and to reject the opportunity now for the first time presented to it.

The words are those of Professor Charles Raven in 1933. We are tempted to ask whether anything wiser has been said on this subject since, and invite the reader to ask how the 'anti' arguments of Part III measure up to this.

Raven and his colleagues did not, of course, win the day, though this statement, and other contemporary statements, were a formative influence upon those of us who took up the struggle in the late 1960s. But the measure would not have been passed by Synod had not present-day clergy become determined to press the cause once again, in their own terms and their own historical context.[25]

So what drove them to take up the fight today? For younger clergymen who were trained and ordained alongside women deacons, it was the cruelty and anachronism of going on to priesthood and leaving the women behind. Others have simply weighed up the arguments on both sides and found the balance overwhelmingly in favour. But the Synod debate would not actually have been won without some significant shifts in the theological and political perspectives of large swathes of the Church.

These came about through the harsh political circumstances of the 1980s. The comfortable coexistence of a liberal Church and an ostensibly benign liberal state which had prevailed since the 1940s became less and less tenable throughout the present Conservative administration. The *Faith in the City* report of 1985[26] signalled a renewed conflict between Church and state on social and economic policies. The report, four hundred pages long, presented a detailed picture of urban poverty and inner-city decay, and constituted one of the most damning, comprehensive indictments of Thatcherism to appear anywhere.

Increasing numbers of Christians became involved in the peace movement. The deployment of Cruise missiles and other weapons of mass destruction throughout the Falklands and Gulf wars, all met with resistance from sections of the churches. And as more and more Christians came into conflict with government on issues of monetarism, militarism and ecological destruction, they had to come to terms with Christianity's historical complicity in these evils before they could go on to proclaim biblical and post-biblical Testament traditions of resistance. (Christian opposition to the Gulf War provides a pertinent example of this. It was the widely neglected and misunderstood 'just war' teaching, which had been developed over many years by the early Church Fathers and formalised by Aquinas in the thirteenth century, that provided the most rigorous and effective case against military intervention.[27])

So in some respects – though not in all – we can see that the soul-searching among men in the churches is akin to our own in the Christian feminist movement. Just as we were forced to hear and respond to the feminist critique of religion as women's most sinister enemy, so too did some thoughtful men have to confront the fact that while Christianity has within it the seeds of liberation, it has more often functioned to maintain evil and oppressive systems.

This is the underlying premiss and starting point of the theology known as Liberation Theology, which came into prominence in the early 1980s. Born amidst resistance to the violent and oppressive dictatorships of Central and South America, Liberation Theology sees deep historical/inspirational parallels between the priority given to social justice in Old Testament and Marxist thought. (Marx, deeply influenced by the Bible, was not quite the 'secularist' he himself and others thought he was.)[28]

Liberationist perspectives encountered hostile resistance from the Christian New Right, who set out to discredit disarmers and lefties generally; this they did by presenting themselves as true adherents of the faith battling against those who would 'water it down' with 'ephemeral' programmes of social action.

Before we examine the impact of this conflict upon our own struggle, we must say something about that old chestnut 'religion and politics'. Few Christians seriously believe that they should – or can – be free of 'secular' influences. We are all commanded to preach the Gospel to the world, and this clearly cannot be done by keeping entirely apart from it: even those who live enclosed lives do so in order to pray more effectively for the world. Indeed, it is often said that the Church is the only organisation that exists for those outside. As we indicated in Part I, the Church of England lays claim to this identity in very specific terms, but it arises in a more general way from the Gospel imperative to love and serve our neighbour. Furthermore, both the Old and New Testaments understand that God works not just through a particular community of believers but through creation and history, and hence through the social movements history throws up – like feminism.

It is vital, therefore, to realise that it was only comparatively recently that a disengagement between religion and politics was deemed possible. As the *Faith in the City* report asserts:

The history of Christianity shows that the very notion of a 'private' religion, without social and political implications, is a relatively modern one: it was only

– 68 –

with the individualistic humanism of the Renaissance, and subsequently with the Cartesian distinction between the thinking soul and the web of material and social phenomena which surround it, that it became possible, and eventually popular, to think of religion as essentially a matter between an individual and God, without regard to the society in which that individual is set.[29]

Conflict between Christians arises, in fact, not over whether individuals or the institution should be 'political', but over what kind of 'politics' Christians should pursue. Membership of the Conservative Party has never been labelled a sell-out to secularism in the way that feminism and socialism have. The political context in which the culture versus faith argument has been worked out over the last twenty years has been one of belligerent conservatism. This, however, has had one advantage: it has made it necessary for the Christian Left to defend the influence of 'secular' ideas more vigorously and cogently, and although this by no means led them to take feminism on board with the liberationist cargo, it has opened up some new trade routes between the two.

The year 1985 saw a theological initiative which had quite direct implications for the Church in Britain. The Kairos Report[30] was produced by the churches in South Africa, a country whose political predicament derives from Britain's own colonial past. In Church terms, too, it was particularly relevant: South Africa also has a 'state Church' (the Dutch Reformed Church) which has, like the Church of England, played a prominent role in shaping national consciousness.

Kairos (a Greek word) means 'the time', but unlike linear time [chronos], kairos is a time in which action is opportune and necessary, as it clearly was in South Africa during the second half of the 1980s. Kairos is a constant theme in the Bible, where it is envisioned not so much in terms of

God inspiring people to take up new opportunities when they arise but as God actually creating opportunities for new life in the Church.

Feminist supporters of women's ordination have taken a strong hold on the idea of kairos and on the description, set out in the Report, of the Church's past, present and potential role in struggles for equality. The Report outlines three theologies: (1) state theology; (2) Church theology; and (3) prophetic theology. The first, 'state theology', sees the Church as the spiritual wing of the state and its role as one of upholding the state's programmes – either in an effort to reform or – as is more often the case – to maintain the status quo. 'Church theology' claims a more independent role for the Church: it envisages a particular obligation to champion, as well as minister to, the needs of oppressed groups. However, it sees the Church's task in terms of peace and reconciliation rather than in structural analysis, and so it 'tends to make use of absolute principles like reconciliation, negotiation, non-violence and peaceful solutions and applies them indiscriminately and uncritically to all situations'. The third, prophetic theology, demands that the Church itself be both an advocate *and an instrument* of change.

The first two approaches can be clearly discerned in past and present responses to women's demands. The hostile stance some Church leaders have adopted towards feminism has, as we have seen, extended to opposing government as well as Church moves towards 'equal rights'. More common today is the second approach, exemplified in Pope John XXIII's statement[31] that the Church should welcome and respond to women's growing consciousness of their human dignity. But in the interests of 'reconciliation' and 'peaceful solutions', any concrete change, particularly within the Church itself, is resisted. It is in the third option – that the Church itself should become an instrument of rather than a responder to change – that we invest our hope for the future.

We were heartened, therefore, by the fact that it was convincingly and eloquently represented in the Synod debate. Bishop Roy Williamson declared himself 'compelled by what I perceive to be the cause of justice'. When bishops and clergy speak of justice, they customarily go on to remind us – as if we did not know – that there are matters of greater moment than this. But we also know from experience that the old 'more pressing concerns' argument is a convenient way of marginalising women's concerns. Williamson put the question into true perspective by asking what the Church existed for. It was founded solely and primarily to bring about the Kingdom, the 'new deal' foretold by the prophets and wrought by Christ for all humanity, whose hallmark is justice. Jesus said that if we 'seek first the kingdom of God and his righteousness', everything else falls into place: 'all other things shall be added unto you' (Matthew 6:33). And so, as Williamson said, 'just as the New Testament bids us have as high a doctrine of ministry as we like, as long as our doctrine of the Church is higher, so it commands us to have as high a doctrine of the Church as we may, provided our doctrine of the Kingdom is higher'.[32]

Although Bishop Williamson, an Irishman, had been more fully exposed to violence and injustice than most of his Synod colleagues, they too had not been unaffected by the deteriorating condition of the underclass in 1980s Britain. As we have already suggested, conflicts with government have – albeit indirectly – influenced thinking on this question: 'High Church' clergy who had previously voted for progressive/radical motions on South Africa, the Bomb, or whatever, but against women, were no longer doing so. That we seem to owe as much to Thatcherism as to our own endeavours in sharpening up the Church's liberal Left does not dismay us. New ideas and the courage to pursue them come to each of us through our own experience. From our own perspective as feminist laywomen, we would like to say that claiming women's priesthood in the late 1980s and early 1990s was a fundamentally different experience from the 1970s campaign. Then, it seemed, we were asking the Church to 'catch up with' feminism and the arguments were inevitably weighted towards the changes women had already brought about in the modern world. In the late 1980s it *felt* more like calling upon the Church to be prophetic in a dark time of backlash against women and all oppressed groups.

The local church

Laypeople's most direct experience of the Church and its turmoils occurs at parish level, and it is here, among particular communities in particular places, that the new women priests are working. We might begin by looking at the particular woes and joys women like Kath Burn, Liz Canham and others encountered as they set about their parish ministries. Hostility was to be expected, and was sometimes alarmingly manifest. On her first day in her parish a man told the Reverend Eve Pitts, a black Anglican deacon, that he could not take Communion from a woman. When she asked why, Pitts was told: 'Because women smell of blood'. Suzanne Fageol might well have been guilty of just that, for she was once severely bitten on the hand while offering the cup to a communicant. Eve Pitts' accuser went on to become a close friend who thanked her for helping him to understand 'that a woman can bring as much dignity to a Communion service as a man'. Stories of implacably opposed parishioners 'coming round' when faced with the person, rather than the idea, of a woman priest are the rule rather than the exception, and a number of surveys carried out here and in the USA confirm this gradual acceptance at parish level. So we should say, in answer to the question we posed at the beginning, that women priests are still here because people want them here.[33]

It is as parishioners themselves that women first discover

their calling, and their parish can either affirm or quash the first intimation. As we have seen, Liz Canham's vocation was firmly quashed, and it was this and later experiences – both as a teacher in South Africa and, on her return, in a London school where racial conflict and social deprivation generated resentment towards authority figures – that led her to seek a new kind of community – one that challenged as well as sheltered her.

Such communities today are likely to be those with a strong commitment to lay leadership backed up by a developed programme of lay education. More often than not, this comes about through sheer necessity.

Recession and falling numbers have brought about a decline of the old parochial system which 'ensured that there should be at least one gentleman resident in every parish of the Kingdom'.[34] Team ministries have long replaced the gentleman parson in rural areas, and their clergy are considerably hard put to cover all the villages and outlying areas, and to keep their church buildings open. So there is simply no way, even if they wanted to, that women priests can be seen as buying into the kind of clerical status many people (particularly urban dwellers) still associate with the Tory shires. Most of those old ivy-clad vicarages have long been occupied by an entirely new class of village gentry and, more positively, the 'rediscovery' of the role of the laity means this picture really exists only in fiction.

Most of Britain's clergy work in urban areas. Keeping the parish structures and the clergy in their vicarages, close to their parishioners, has been a major priority – and for very good reasons. In areas of inner-city decay the parish clergy are quite often the only 'professional carers' who have not fled to live in safer, more salubrious parts of town. Urban clergy are uniquely placed witnesses to what is happening to our inner cities, and have prophesied therefrom to good effect with *Faith in the City*, which was compiled from on-the-spot evidence from inner-city clergy and laity.[35] The report noted the contribution already made by women to local life in inner cities, and submitted that women's ordination would be an important way of extending the Church's pastoral care in these beleaguered places.

It has done more, however, than 'recommend'. Church funds and resources are now being consciously targeted towards what the report has defined as Urban Priority Areas (UPAs). Every parish in the land has been called upon to help and support their UPA 'neighbours in need'. Newly ordained women will, of course, be an addition to these resources. How, and what, can we expect them to contribute? The inordinate length of time all this has taken has meant that women ordinands have been stuck on the Church's career ladder. Unable to celebrate the Eucharist – the Church's central act of worship – unassisted women ordinands and deacons have worked mainly in team ministries or in non-parochial ministries like university and hospital chaplaincies. Many of the more senior women deacons are now 'in charge' of parishes within a team ministry but have not, until now, been able to move on to become proper 'vicars' in the traditionally understood sense. On one level this has put them under an enormous disadvantage: they have not been in the position of pastoral oversight – which includes the training of younger clergy – which their skills and experience have merited, and which the Church certainly needs. Against this clear wastage of womanpower, however, we could argue that those who have, through their gender, been deprived of access to 'top jobs' are particularly well placed to help others get a perspective on notions of a career in a Church which may soon, as much from necessity as from a growing conviction that this is a more Christian way of doing things, have far fewer such jobs to offer.

Certainly, British women deacons have already shown considerable adaptability with regard to 'job' sharing and becoming 'worker priests' – that is, ordained people who earn their living at other jobs and offer their 'services' free.

Three women deacons who trained together in the mid 1980s offer an encouraging example of ministry as service (as well as a sound model of the Christian and feminist principle of shared poverty): one of their number wanted to undertake work which carried no salary, so the three decided to split two salaries three ways so that this important job could be done.

A distrust of power exercised by the strong over the weak lies at the heart of the feminist critique of the Church. We have seen something of this distrust expressed by those men who are rejecting state and Church theologies for a more biblical/radical understanding of 'kingdom' (God's rule), and we may see more now that thoughtful men are at least beginning to come to grips with the overwhelmingly sexist and patriarchal nature of the institution.[36] For some of them, as we shall see in Part III, ordaining women is not the answer, but for many more it has become not the whole answer but an important part of the answer.

Why women should be priests: some conclusions

The movement to ordain women originally arose from the clear fact that women feel called to be priests. They feel called not only in the private depths of their souls, but also by the congregations they already serve and by the wider Church which still has need of their talents. The Church has heard their call, as we have said, in a dark time: a time in which it would be foolish to predict the future either of the Church itself or of the women who will serve it as priests.

Who twenty years ago – when the present round of this campaign began – or a hundred years ago – when the demise of religion as a force in nation-building seemed certain in the West – could have predicted the worldwide rise in religious fundamentalism? Where it will lead we cannot tell, and it would be arrogant as well as far beyond the scope of this book to try to pass judgement on its non-Christian forms. But since we do know that it represents one of the most serious threats to women's well-being and autonomy the modern world has seen, we cannot, as religious people, detach ourselves from the plight of women who live under the shadow of patriarchal theocracy – not because, like us, they choose to, but because they are forced to. And we do know something about the Christian congregations which have gone in this direction. They too are heavily male-dominated in terms of leadership (though not, of course, in terms of numbers – women shoulder a heavy load of the real work). Leadership is very much 'top–down', and the leaders themselves are prone to see 'success' in terms of numbers – 'bums on pews'! Some of these churches, however, are those in which women have long been able to be ministers, and there is evidence that these women are strenuously resisting the trend towards autocracy. They do so by working in a more traditionally pastoral way – not by bringing people into the Church but by ministering to them where and as they are. 'It's the woman minister people on the estate [near one of these fundamentalist churches] actually know. They trust her because she cares for them as people, not as "pew fodder",' one observer remarked.[37]

The call to be 'with God, with *all* people on your heart' is one that has sustained women ordinands of all denominations. Can we hope, then, that Anglican women priests will add reinforcements to the fight against conservatism and misogyny that seem so deeply entrenched in our society? We are far from happy with our own Church's cultural and political establishment, but it might prove an advantage here. That the state Church, whose mandate is to serve all, has now endorsed the pastoral and representative authority of women cannot be a disadvantage.

But arguments for the ordination of women do not rest just on negatives. The Church itself needs women priests to make itself whole again, in order to reflect, as McLaughlin puts it:

> a more ample, a more Catholic vision of what the church and her mission to a broken world can be . . . For those who have never imagined or seen a woman in a position of juridical presidency there will be a sense of innovation, but not if one knows the history of the old church . . . what seems to be new – a woman at the altar – actually at a deeper level may be the recovery of an old treasure, that is, the more adequate and richer imaging of God by female as well as male 'icons', which the old church achieved in one way, we today in a different situation, in another.[38]

Our very different situation is one in which the Christian Church itself is marginalised. We are heartened by the changes we have charted here, and we fervently believe that if sexism could be eradicated from the Christian Church, patriarchy would lose much of its force. This is why we also believe that this whole debate is indeed of interest to all women. But we cannot delude ourselves that the Church has any more than a symbolic power. It exists in most people's minds to console, to make human a brutal and coercive world; so to all political intents and purposes the Church occupies a place in the world remarkably akin to that which most women occupy. So our most real – and therefore our dearest – hope is that Christian feminism as a whole, and this campaign in particular, has helped people inside and outside the churches to connect their experience of marginalisation in more meaningful ways. As Margaret Miles suggests:

> The intense cumulative process by which women come to know – and say – what they think, listen to the perspectives of other women, and develop analyses, critiques and plans for social action can occur in the context of a space that is simultaneously public and,

in a post-Christian society, sheltered by its marginalisation. Christian churches . . . could re-discover an ancient religious role of providing a counter-cultural prophetic voice in relation to the values and interests of secular culture.[39]

How women priests will develop their own authentic counter-cultural voice remains to be seen.

PART THREE

---◆---

. . . And Those Against

ALTHOUGH THE CENTURY of struggle charted in Part II did indeed bring many people to the point where the ordination of women seemed natural, inevitable and just, it equally brought many others to defensive battle stations.

What they thought they were defending varied very considerably from one group to another; opposition was by no means uniformly of one complexion. Some were quite obviously simply defending the Church's right to go on being a 'safe haven' for male dominance; but others, more seriously, were defending their understanding of historical truth, or their vision of Church unity, or even their belief in freedom and equality for women. Some opposed this *specific* legislation as presented for Synod to vote on; as we shall see, it was a tortuous and difficult proposal, and by no means the ideal vehicle for change.

But one thing is striking: all groups in the run-up to the Church of England's decision took for granted a decidedly 'untraditional' view of the roles of women and men. The Enlightenment assumptions about the basic equality of all people were accepted, at least in theory, by both sides, and we must reiterate, as we have already stressed so far, that this is a *novel* view in the long history of Christianity. It does not, of course, lead to easy practical conclusions, since equality cannot mean being identical, so there is always room for interpretation along the 'equal but different' line. This was said, not least, by feminist critics of the movement for women's ordination, and it is to this group that we turn first.

Liberating women?

Feminists have a number of different reasons for being dubious about the ordination of women. Some, who might not be actively opposed to the priesting of women are still impatient at the time and energy that have been expended on what is, to them, a rather minor issue. This attitude is not, of course, limited to feminist opponents of women's ordination; it has been one of the standard ways of belittling the issue: 'Hasn't the Church got anything better to do with its time?' Few supporters of November's motion would quibble with that – they have, indeed, said as much themselves. It was hardly their doing that the whole process has taken decades rather than years, and most of them would now hope to lend their powers to the other things the Church should indeed be doing. But there is no doubt that far too much of the Church's lifeblood has been poured into this issue over the last decade. Whole swathes of the Church are now to be identified only by whether they are 'pro' or 'anti'. The 'catholic' wing of the Church of England, for example, which used to be known for its pioneering presence in areas of urban decay and social deprivation, is now – in the eyes of outsiders, at least – campaigning only to keep women out of the priesthood. The many catholics who were converted to 'feminism' on the grounds of Gospel justice are often forgotten.

Firm supporters of women's ordination – many of whom, as we saw in Part II, have given virtually the whole of their adult lives to the cause – have done so in the firm belief that this issue *relates*, and that the struggle for justice in this one area will actually have repercussions in others. But it is precisely this that many feminists deny. As we saw in Part II, there are still those who support the ordination of women without supporting any further extension of feminism within the Church, and their denial that the ordination of women had anything to do with the struggle against sexism fuels feminist suspicion.

Some feminists feel even more strongly that nothing, in heaven or on earth, will make the Church non-sexist. For them, the problem with the ordination of women is not that it is a waste of the *Church's* time but that it is a waste of *women's* time. A writer like, for example, Daphne Hampson[1] argues that it is not just an accident of history that the Church is a sexist institution: its sexism is an inevitable result of its doctrine of God. If that were indeed the case, then she would be right in saying that the struggle to ordain women is just tinkering round the edges of the problem. The problem itself would be soluble only by abandoning Christianity altogether. Why waste energy struggling with a moribund institution when the future lies in a search for an authentically woman-centred spirituality that has not been formed by male religious aspirations?

Hampson's argument has real bite for feminists, and its critique of Christianity cannot be dismissed as that of an 'outsider'. Hampson spent years working for the ordination of women; indeed, for some time she was convinced that her own future lay in the ordained ministry of the Church. Quite apart from the theological and moral seriousness of her work, the sheer pain that the Church inflicted on her through years of rejection must be taken as a real question mark against the Church's ability to care for women. We have already seen how hurt is an inevitable part of a woman ordinand's path in the Church at the moment. Must it not, then, be a genuine alternative to reject an institution that is so stacked – theologically, historically, institutionally and temperamentally – against the female sex? As Hampson herself succinctly puts it:

The challenge of feminism is not simply that women wish to gain an equal place with men in what is essentially a religion which is biased against them. The challenge of feminism is that women may want to express their understanding of God within a different thought structure . . . While men (and some women) consider whether women can be full insiders within the church, women debate whether or not they want to be.[2]

She simply assumes that the ordination debate is not one that any intelligent woman would want to pursue.

Hampson's reasons for rejecting Christianity have a powerful emotional pull for most Christian feminists, but they are seriously weakened by her ahistorical method and by her unwillingness to apply her critique of Christianity to other issues. Though she – quite rightly – treats sexism as a primary source of oppression, she does not analyse how sexism connects with other forms of oppressive behaviour, such as racism and classism.[3]

We hope that we have at least begun to address the central question that Hampson poses to Christian feminists: why stay in such a damaging religion? We have tried to show how sexism is a distortion – as is racism – of Christianity's vision of 'the Kingdom of God', and we have also tried to show how women have continued to find Christianity a source of nourishment, and a voice for speaking the truths of liberation to our still-deaf society. But how far women priests will help to address Hampson's critique of Christianity remains to be seen.

Certainly, many opponents of women's ordination have fallen upon the work of Hampson and other post-Christian feminists with glee. They brandish it aloft as proof that what women ordinands really want to do is radically to change the face of Christianity, working from inside to undermine the whole edifice. Some have brought out the old chestnut that women priests bring about a return to a pagan 'goddess' ethos, as though to change the sex of the minister is automatically to change the religion, irrespective of what the minister actually does.

Even some supporters of women's ordination have made this strange assumption. Tony Grist, for example, writing in the *Guardian*'s 'Face to Faith' column, informs us – in ecstatically approving tones – that the goddess, who has never really been away, is returning 'within the Christian church. The Anglican decision to ordain women is superficially about equal opportunities, fundamentally about this profound change in Western theology.' No proof is given of this assertion, and it reeks strongly of the old pre-Enlightenment view of women as incapable of being – or unwilling to be, *in themselves*, without male support – Christian.

When such absurdities are taken to be typical of all women ordinands, they can do great damage. A writer like William Oddie, for example, by implying that all feminist theologians are saying essentially the same thing, attempted to frighten the ecclesiastical horses into believing that the ordination of women would bring about the death of God. *What Will Happen to God?*, his book title plaintively demanded, as though only he and a few like-minded heroes stood between God and the monstrous regiment of feminists.[4]

How very far from the truth these notions of a 'takeover bid' are has already been demonstrated in Part II. The experiences of ordained women, either in the Anglican Church abroad or in denominations that have had women ministers for years, suggest that they have not yet dented sexism deeply, either in theory or in practice.[5] Women ministers are, predominantly, in lower-paid, lower-status jobs. It seems that we face at least years, and possibly decades, with men still 'at the top'. So some feminists, who do not wish to follow Hampson's example and leave the Church, are still very doubtful whether the ordination of women is in fact a liberating thing. They wonder if a two-tier clerical system does not actually set back, rather than promote, the equality of women. Sara Maitland has argued that 'it is more undermining for women's self image to have an "inferior priest" around than none at all'.[6] And if that is true, then to retain the unique insider–outsider stance that has been ours for so long – belonging to the Church, yet also challenging it with the greater freedom of the feminist movement outside – might well be a more valuable thing: to remain 'prophets', rather than selling ourselves for the mess of pottage that the priesthood appears in such a scheme of things – just a 'small gain from a bankrupt bureaucracy'.[7]

This point is also made powerfully by the American Catholic feminist writer Elizabeth Schussler Fiorenza. She argues that all public institutions are still so dominated by male characteristics that women who wish to 'participate actively in this male-determined world must adapt themselves to men'.[8] And this is no less true of the priesthood than of any other institutional office. But nowadays, it is not necessarily a feminist goal to be able to be 'like a man'. Instead, women are celebrating and discovering what it is like to be a woman, and it is very unclear that priesthood is as yet a vehicle for doing that. Similarly, Schussler Fiorenza has suggested that women should not start a campaign for admission to 'the lowest rung of the hierarchical ladder'.[9] Instead, they should start by campaigning to be admitted to offices of power and prestige, since the role models younger women need are not those of subservience but those of achievement.

In theory, of course, these points carry great conviction, but they are outweighed, we believe, by another basic tenet of feminist theory: that it is women's *experience* that must become the standpoint from which we challenge society. And it is undeniable that in this whole debate about the priesting of women, it is the *experience* of the women who, against all odds, felt themselves called to the priesthood, both inwardly – subjectively – and outwardly, by the local churches they served, that has proved the most compelling argument. It is the *experience* of people like Una Kroll, Liz Canham, Kath Burn and Eleanor McLaughlin that should demand support from feminists, even feminists who have theoretical doubts about the institution to which their sisters feel called.[10]

The hope of convincing unconvinced feminists that the

ordination of women to the priesthood is really a liberating symbol lies with future generations of women priests, and with those men who have seen feminism as one of the transformative symbols for the justice and equality of God. If, indeed, it were possible to embody the vision of change in an institutional form, that would be a deeply heartening experience. Surely it is better to travel hopefully than not to travel at all, if you have a longed-for destination.

Women Against the Ordination of Women

But of course, not all women who oppose the ordination of women do so on the grounds that the move is not sufficiently feminist. Many Christian women have been opposed on the grounds that women's ordination is a sell-out to secular contemporary views of women. They point out that our society actually has no coherent understanding of the proper relations between men and women, so it is trying to pretend that 'equal' must mean 'interchangeable'. These women, like the feminists mentioned above, suggest that if women are ordained to the priesthood, the Church will have passed up a perfect opportunity to explore what the ministry of women might really be. All that will happen is that a male ministry will be offered by women, and will lose the safe sanctity of its traditional male form without seriously benefiting either women or the Church.

There is a serious point here. The Church has always tended to undervalue 'ministries' that are not part of the hierarchy. Indeed, in many people's minds 'the Church' simply means its building and its vicar. For example, when people say 'The Church should speak out', they usually mean its top-ranking clergy, and the question of women's ordination is often posed as one about whether women should 'go into the Church' – as though they were not there already.

There is also a danger that the work of laypeople like ourselves is not thought of as 'real' Church work, and therefore that active laywomen will be acceptable to WAOW, whereas their ordained sisters are not. But we are laypeople not because we have accepted a 'womanly' role, but because our vocation is different. Certainly, all kinds of lay roles should be explored and expanded, but only in a context in which ordination is one possibility among many for all Christians. It is only when the whole range of possibilities is open to women that they can discover which one they are really called to.

Much of the literature produced by the organisation 'Women Against the Ordination of Women' opposes different kinds of women. On the one hand, there are 'nice' women, like Mother Teresa; on the other, there are 'pushy' women, like those who wish to be ordained. Mother Teresa's obvious strength and force of personality are not bars to her being 'nice' because she is theoretically conservative about the role of women in society, and limits herself to a 'serving' role, albeit one requiring tremendous toughness as well as compassion. This kind of argument rather gives the game away: WAOW see priesthood largely in terms of *power*, of an outward, hierarchical kind that women should not want or need. It would – indeed, should – be possible to describe priesthood in terms of just the very kind of compassion and service that should make it more natural for women rather than men to be priests. That priesthood has not been performed in this way is a judgement on the historical priesthood, not on the women who now feel called to be priests.

WAOW literature extends its dubious thesis by pointing to the great women of the past who were happy to serve the Church without priesthood. They have, of course, had to choose their examples rather carefully. As we have seen, Thérèse of Lisieux, who has been held up by the Church as a model of womanly humility, longed to be a priest. Florence Nightingale has actually been used in WAOW posters, but Nightingale's own writings tell us that she turned to nursing not so much because her heart overflowed with womanly tenderness as because the Church would not use her gifts in any formal way.

The fact that, as we saw in Part II, priesthood was not an option for women before this century is not mentioned by WAOW, though, of course, feminist scholars who claim women of the past as 'proto-feminists' are guilty of just as much anachronistic ahistoricism. Women of the past cannot be made to speak directly either for or against the motion in this debate, since the question was not theirs. We might wish to cite the authority claimed by women such as Teresa of Avila or Catherine of Siena – both were fearless in their opposition to the male hierarchy when it countermanded their own divine prompting. They did not claim priestly authority or 'natural' authority, only the authority of their calling by God. Both were very much women of their time, seeing themselves as dutiful daughters of the Church, yet convinced of God's gift through them to the Church.

This does not constitute proof that they would have wanted to be priests if they were alive today. That is to enter into the realms of fantasy. But the kind of authority they claimed is clearly not in line with some of the appeals to women's 'special' nature or 'essential' difference that are employed by numbers of opponents of women's ordination, who suggest that the role given to women within Christianity is so special, so important, that we should 'leave the men their priesthood':

> To those women who truly do feel that they are called to the priesthood I should like to say something speaking just as a woman . . . Remember that we have surely been given the greatest gift of all and been immensely blessed by God in that a woman was the mother of Christ.

> His own mother Mary, in her obedience and humility, offers an unbeatable role model for women for all time.[11]

All of this suggests that women serve only *as women* – that is, as creatures who must always serve through their biological gifts. It seems to be saying that God gives womankind, as a whole, as a gift to the Church, but that women can bring *only* their 'womanliness', not their particular, individual gifts. Christian history seems to make a nonsense of this assertion as does the Christian Gospel. Women are not called to be Mary to men's Christ. All Christians are called to be 'in Christ'.

What is more, sweeping statements about the imitation of Mary are very hard to translate into practicalities. Why is it all right for women to run campaigning organisations like WAOW in the Church, but not to be priests? Why is the one 'obedient and humble' and the other not? And who is this 'humble' Mary, anyway? In St Luke's Gospel, Mary rejoices over her pregnancy because by carrying God incarnate in her womb she is helping to show what kind of a God this is: 'he has scattered the proud', 'he has put down the mighty', 'he has filled the hungry with good things, and the rich he has sent empty away' (Luke 1: 46–55). Obedience like this Mary's might not produce the results that WAOW intend.

Absolutists and multilateralists

So there are good – though not, we believe, overriding – feminist reasons for opposing women's ordination, and there are bad reasons, based on an 'essentialist' position about the nature of women. Some of the reasons given for *not* ordaining women either show such a heretical doctrine of God, or are so clearly fuelled by dislike and distrust of women, that they have actually proved counterproductive and become arguments *for* ordaining women.

If, for example, the case for keeping the priesthood male relies so heavily on the symbolic significance of the *maleness* of Christ that women are actually excluded from his saving work,[12] then that becomes a reason for ordaining women, to recover the traditional understanding that Christ's humanity and his salvation are universally inclusive. Or, again, if the argument goes that whatever the claims of justice, the Church's need for priests, and the missionary potential of women priests in the modern world, all the same, the Church must maintain the priesthood exactly as it was in the past or God will refuse to honour its sacraments, that again functions as a reason to ordain women. Would a God who became incarnate in a human being, and permitted himself to be put to a horrible death simply so that people could know his love, *really* then impose such tight conditions about how the sacraments of that love are to be administered?

Some of the less obviously dubious theology about the different callings of women and men actually has an unwished-for outcome as well. It is very hard to see how one can justify allowing women to do everything else, including the exercise of all kinds of authority, teaching, personal and pastoral, while keeping only the eucharistic as a male preserve. Theologies of the priesthood have to become so convoluted and untraditional to achieve this particular 'line in the sand' that, once more, one cannot help feeling that ordaining women is the lesser of two evils. In particular, when women ordinands are faced, as they are, with male priests who can, apparently, live with women priests and ministers – either in other denominations or, even more illogically, in other Anglican churches – provided they, personally, don't ever have to work with them, or acknowledge their priesthood, then one cannot help suspecting that this is misogyny masquerading as theology.

Having said all that, however, some of the objections to the ordination of women have real ecclesiological roots, rather than simply sexist ones. That is, they are to do with beliefs about the nature of the Church and its well-being. We have already argued, in Part I, that some of these are in fact dependent upon the non-traditional belief about women as 'equal but different', though this is seldom spelled out. Others merely reflect a deep incoherence about what *kind* of a decision it is to admit women to the priesthood: is it an issue that affects the fundamentals of Christian faith, or is it just a matter of local church legislation? This confusion is not limited to opponents of the ordination of women, as we shall see.

One group of opponents to the ordination of women are those who believe that it will *always* be wrong to ordain women to the priesthood, since this is contrary to 'Scripture and tradition'. The majority of Evangelical opponents of women's ordination would fit into this category, since they base their opposition to the move on their understanding of the relationship between women and men that they see described in Scripture. Their position is a particularly delicate one now, since they could not easily find a home in the Roman Catholic Church if they found themselves unable to live under the Church of England's new regulations, and most of the 'Protestant' denominations in Britain already have women ministers. Although their plight has received far less attention in the media than that of people like Anne Widdecombe, who has left the Church of England to join the Church of Rome, they are, in fact, left with far fewer options than those from the 'catholic' wing of the Church of England.

Both the Roman Catholic and the Orthodox churches might provide a temporary home for those from the High Church end of the Church of England who believe that women can never be admitted to the priesthood. We say 'temporary' because, as Anne Widdecombe herself admitted in a recent speech,[13] they may find it necessary to move on again when their new Church admits women to the priesthood. While there is no immediate likelihood of Rome admitting women priests, the groundswell of support among American and British Roman Catholics in particular cannot be denied. Very few Roman Catholic theologians are prepared to defend the 'traditional' position on women priests, and although they are highly unlikely to sway the present Pope, who knows what the future holds? Certainly, when the Roman Catholic Church decides to ordain women, the process it will go through will be far simpler than the one the Church of England has had to endure, and there will be no talk of 'alternative episcopal oversight', since the Church of Rome is not prone to doubt its right to speak for the universal Church, or the authority of its statements.

The Eastern Orthodox churches provide a more enduring home for those who are opposed to women's ordination, since discussion of the question is in its infancy in many of these churches, and not even conceived in others. But their historical and ethnic differences with the Western churches make them a less obvious resource to the majority of Anglican malcontents, though there are some who are considering Orthodoxy as a real option to be actively explored.

Certainly, those who oppose the ordination of women on the grounds that it can *never* be right must face the possibility that they and their successors will have to move from Church to Church for ever, ending up in some small sect of their own devising, the last remaining 'true' Church. For them, it would be no recommendation that the whole of Christendom had agreed to ordain women – they would have to part company with Christendom. As Mary Gordon says in connection with another great traditionalist, Cardinal Marcel Lefebvre: 'he values obedience to authority and connection to tradition so highly that when he sees the Church breaking with tradition he breaks with the Church'.[14]

Although a few members of the Church of England have already left to join other churches, the majority are still waiting to see if a satisfactory formula can be reached to allow 'traditionalists' to remain. There might be any number of reasons for this – loyalty to the Church that formed them, trust in the hierarchy, hope that November 1992's decision will finally be invalidated: all these would be good reasons for holding fire. But it is also possible that large numbers of those opponents remaining in the Church of England are those who believe not that it is *impossible* that women should be priests, merely that it is *impolitic* at the moment.

Some of these people see the ordination of women as 'the last straw' in a growing pile of liberal straws. They would cite the new Prayer Book, the toleration of 'liberal' theology and the Christian feminist movements as symptoms of the Church's unfortunate compromise with secular thought. But is there any real, theological connection between the ordination of women and the other bitter pills that are said to have been administered? David Martin, one of the founder members of The Prayer Book Society, which was formed to campaign for the continuing use of the old liturgy in the Church of England, certainly doubts it. He has recently resigned from the society in protest at their decision to oppose the ordination of women, since – in his eyes, at least – a love of traditional liturgy need not go hand in hand with a wider kind of 'conservatism-for-its-own-sake' in the Church.

Equally, of course, the reverse is true: it is possible to be in favour of all kinds of other changes in the Church, without having any interest in feminist issues. The male generic forms in the new Alternative Service Books are clear proof that liturgical reforms were not guided by any spirit of feminism, and the same is true of 'liberal' theology in general. Monica Furlong has pointed out that it is still possible to write a book entitled *Christology in Modern Times*, and even win a prize for it, 'apparently totally unaware of any of the questions being asked by feminists about Christology'.[15] The Roman Catholic Church has undertaken similar liturgical reforms, yet it is seen as a possible home by those who object to the Church of England. So it is hard not to scent a certain amount of disingenuousness in those who say that women priests are only one of a number of sources of unease.

Those, on the other hand, who say that it may well be God's will to have women priests, but this is not something the Church of England should decide on its own, are putting forward a rather more serious point: the 'multilateralist' point. 'Multilateralist' opponents of women's ordination argue that the kind of disunity introduced into the Church's ministry by allowing women to minister in one part of a Church and not others is theologically unacceptable. We have already indicated in Part I that we see this as a serious point. How can a bishop function as a 'focus of unity' if the bishop's clergy are not all in communion with him or her? But the sad fact of the matter is that the Christian Church is *not* united. Quite apart from the fact that the post-Reformation Church is divided into more than five hundred sects, which do not present any great picture of unity, even those symbols of unity shared by the traditional churches are also already broken, long before women priests come on to the scene. The Church is supposed to be 'the body of Christ', but it operates as a number of different bodies. Mutual love between Christians is supposed to be so striking that outsiders cannot help noticing it, but in fact, different Christian denominations will often speak to *anyone* but each other.

This is not, of course, an argument for wantonly introducing further disunity into the Church, but it does suggest that there are some questions where the Church must stand up for what is perceived to be the truth, whatever the cost. And in the particular instance of the ordination of women, the issue is further complicated by the fact that what seems to put more barriers between the Church of England and the Roman Catholic and Orthodox churches actually *promotes* unity of ministries between the Church of England and other churches, some Anglican and some of other denominations, that already ordain women. So it is not straightforwardly a case of introducing diversity where previously there was uniformity. Within the Anglican churches it may actually create a better impression of unity, since women priests from abroad will now be able to function in Britain in the same way as their male colleagues. How far this inter-Anglican Unity will be marred by 'no-go' areas for women priests remains to be seen, since it is still not clear how many opponents of women priests will choose to remain within the Church of England over the next few years.

So the undoubted force of the 'multilateralist' view on the unity of the Church is slightly lessened by the fact that it seldom acknowledges the reality of already existing Church divisions. It is also often framed with surprising insularity, as though Anglican relations with the Church of Rome and with Orthodoxy are affected *only* by what the Church of England chooses to do. In fact, of course, inter-Church dialogues are held between the Anglican Church as a whole and other churches. The Anglican–Roman Catholic conversations (ARCIC), for example, have continued throughout the decade, despite the fact that the Anglican Church has had women priests for the whole of this period. So in fact, unity with other churches, even if it was immediately possible, would *already* have to consider Anglican women priests, before there are any at all in England.

After all, the Church of England is a latecomer to women's ordination among Anglican churches, so that those who feel compelled to leave – or, at the very least, dispute the Church's authority – should have done so when the first women were ordained. An unwillingness to recognise that change has already occurred does, again, lead to a suspicion about motives. It becomes not so much an ecclesiological issue as simply a desire not to allow 'our own patch' to be affected.

But there is a further question that must be asked of these 'multilateralists'. What is it about *this* question – the ordination of women – that makes it one a local Church must not tackle alone? To say that it is a decision that the Anglican Church should not take alone is to imply that it *is* one that a more fully united Church could take – in other words, that it is not a matter of such fundamental significance that it would change the nature of Christianity. It is not, for example, on a par with the belief that Jesus is both divine and human, and that his Incarnation has saving consequences for the human race. These beliefs are non-negotiable; the question of the ordination of women, for 'multilateralists', does not seem to be in that league. In that sense, can it be described as a question about 'order' – how a church regulates itself – rather than about 'faith' – things that are common to all Christians? Decisions about order concern the day-to-day administration of the Church, and may change to suit local and historical situations. An example of this kind of decision might be the Roman Catholic Church's practice of dictating that all clergy must be celibate.

So is the ordination of women a question of 'faith' or a question of 'order'? If it is a question of faith, then a change can never be made by any church, and there can be no such thing as 'multilateralism' on the question. If it is a matter of 'order', then it is one that a provincial church, like the Church of England, is perfectly entitled to decide on its own, and it is hard to see why it should have caused such uproar. Those who oppose the ordination of women on the grounds that we should wait for greater unity on the question must seriously consider whether there is any other decision about 'order' that would require a similar unanimity. If not, they are obviously working with some prior understanding of the proper place of women in the Church that is actually dictating the terms. We are back to the kinds of questions that were raised in Part I: unless it can be argued that the priesthood *must* be changed in being exercised by women, it is hard to see how this can be a question of 'faith' rather than simply one of 'order'.

This point is not, of course, one that operates only in one direction. As Bishop William Wantland from America has pointed out:

The 1976 canon was simply permissive. No one was forced to accept women in the priesthood . . . [But] even though the canon has been declared simply permissive, there are now a growing number of radicals who are insisting on a mandatory interpretation of the canon.[16]

Bishop Wantland, Bishop of Eau Claire, USA, is one of the continuing 'traditionalists' in the Episcopal Church of America, and his paper is written to encourage English 'traditionalists' to seek statutory, rather than merely synodical, guarantees of their position. He reminds us that while opponents of women priests were 'protected' when the ordination measure was first passed in Canada, that protection was not legally enshrined, and has now been allowed to lapse. The Canadian Church seems to have assumed that the period in which it was acceptable to hold a different opinion about women's ordination is now over.

The point the Bishop is making, however, is that if this really is a decision about 'order' rather than 'faith', then no one can be *required* to believe it. It cannot be taken as one of the marks of a Christian. It is on these grounds that November 1992's legislation enshrined the right of opponents to remain within the Church of England. But Bishop Wantland is speaking from a Church that has experienced women's priestly ministry for nearly twenty-five years, and is beginning, he believes, to feel that there is no room for continuing dissent on the issue.

But how is a church to decide when something has sufficient support to be adopted as the only policy operating for that church? Must it wait for every single opponent to be converted – which will surely not happen this side of heaven, on any question whatsoever? Will a two-thirds majority do? Apparently not, according to the opponents of November 1992's decision in Synod. Bishop Wantland cites, in his defence, a document produced on behalf of all the Anglican churches, which says:

> The fact that a synod has reached a decision does not foreclose the matter. Both sides need to work hard . . . recognizing that synodical decisions may indeed

come to be overwhelmingly affirmed, or on the other hand equally as overwhelmingly rejected.[17]

But who decides what is 'overwhelming'? The basic assumption is that at some point in the future members of the Church will know whether or not they were right to ordain women to the priesthood. Who decides when this point has been reached?

Bishop Wantland's pamphlet was produced in Britain under the auspices of a group called Cost of Conscience. Like the Movement for the Ordination of Women in this respect, if no other, Cost of Conscience is an umbrella organisation. It represents catholics and evangelicals, multilateralists and absolutists; for this reason, its campaigning force has been somewhat diminished in its post-November 1992 incarnation as Forward in Faith. Some of its members have already left the Church of England: some after Parliament ratified Synod's decision; and others are still waiting to see if the bishops will emerge with some kind of package that will enable them to stay within the Church of England.

As we said at the beginning of this book, any deal that can be struck with opponents of the ordination of women will profoundly affect the ways in which women priests will be able to operate, as well as how they are perceived. Although we have been focusing upon the ecclesiological aspects of the question, there is also an ethical dimension to the Church's current negotiations. If we transfer the discussion to another historical context, the anomaly is clearer. Should the government have contemplated compensating those with a deeply held conviction of their right to hold slaves after the Abolition vote in the 1830s? Or would the Church now contemplate 'compensation' for those who did not wish to share the priesthood with black people? If the Church genuinely believes – as its Synod vote should suggest – that there are no overwhelming theological objections to women's ordination, and if it is the claims of justice that have brought many people to accept this vote, then how can the Church really make room for those who oppose it?

We shall argue that there are strong reasons for doing so, but as we go on to look at the practical steps being taken to safeguard opponents of women priests, we do so against the background of belief that the comparison with the race issue is one that such opponents have yet to answer.

November 1992 and its aftermath

The members of General Synod who voted on the question of the ordination of women in November 1992 had, on the whole, been elected to do just that. Although General Synod has had a mass of other business to process in the current sitting, elections to Synod were fought very largely on what the proposed candidates' views were on 'the women question'.

By the time members of Synod went in to vote on Wednesday 11 November, both sides had done their sums, totting up those known to be on their side and making estimates of the probable voting patterns of waverers. The vote was clearly going to be extremely close, but opponents of the measure were quietly confident that it would just fail to get the necessary two-thirds majority in the House of Laity.

In fact, of course, the measure was passed, but it is highly probable that the end result was due to about two changed votes in the House of Laity, which passed it by what amounted to 67.3 per cent – just squeezing through the two-thirds barrier. That could be accounted for by one person who changed their mind during the course of the debate, and one woman who felt unable to vote at all, and remained, visibly distressed, in the debating chamber as the House divided.

While we must not forget that two-thirds is still a very sizeable majority, the dangerous closeness of the vote made it a particularly devastating blow to opponents of the measure. The emotional and practical disarray of the opposition after the vote suggests that they did not, in fact, believe that the day would finally be lost to them. There were clearly no plans waiting to be put into motion should the vote go against them, and the months that followed the vote have been hard and painful ones for opponents of women priests, as they tried to assess what their position should be in the Church that they perceived to be radically changed by the vote.

But the vote did not come out of the blue. All priests ordained in the last twenty years must have reckoned with the possibility that women would be ordained in their life-time. Clearly, many opponents saw this as, at most, a remote, theoretical proposition, but they cannot deny that it was at least that. Since 1986, however, it has been a real possibility. That was when the first report outlining the scope of the legislation necessary to permit women to be ordained to the priesthood was submitted to Synod. The first women were ordained to the diaconate in 1987, two years after Synod had given final approval for the step.

All the subsequent reports on legislation and financial provision for those who would feel that they must leave the Church were produced by committees that consisted of both supporters and opponents of women's ordination. The intention was to have in place a scheme that would be acceptable to both parties *before* the vote. It is particularly ironic that the legislation was framed, in all its tortuousness, specifically to avoid the kind of wrangling and horse-trading that have been taking place since the vote. Yet even before November 1992, it was clear to all concerned that opponents of the ordination of women would not be happy with the provisions of the legislation. It is almost as if they had hoped that the legislation itself, with its commitment to paying out large sums of money to those who would be forced to leave the Church, would actually prove so frightening to most Synod members that they would vote against it.

If that was the aim, it clearly did not work. Immediately after the vote, many of the details – except the stark ones of payment for the few who instantly knew they would leave – had to be renegotiated. It seems that it would actually have been simpler if Synod had voted just on the issue: should women be priested in the Church of England, or not? The complexities of exactly how this should be done could then have been worked out separately – as, in fact, they are being worked out now.

Instead, Synod had to vote on a package that was both demeaning to the women concerned – in that *from the very beginning* it put their vocations chiefly in the light of the cost to the Church – and, at the same time, left their opponents high and dry. The financial provision would obviously apply only to those who actually left the Church of England. Although the Archbishop of Canterbury assured those who opposed women's ministry but wanted to stay in the Anglican Church after the vote that 'There is certainly no question of those who continue to doubt the theological justification for the priesting of women having any less place within our Church',[18] it was far from clear that the measures framed for them in the legislation would be either acceptable or workable.

Just how a satisfactory compromise could be reached was to be the central question for the Church in the months during which Parliament was considering whether or not to ratify Synod's vote.

The role of the Roman Catholic Church

Many opponents of the measure frankly doubted that the Church of England could find a way of holding such disparate practices together, and for many of them the obvious answer was to turn to another church. Those from the 'catholic' wing of the Church of England began to make overtures to Rome. The retired Bishop of London, Graham Leonard, is reported to have suggested a scheme that would allow dissidents to form their own church, using Anglican worship and under the direction of an Anglican bishop, such as himself, but being 'adopted' into the Roman Catholic Church. This kind of church – sometimes called a 'uniate' church – does exist in certain areas, chiefly in Eastern Europe and the Middle East, where small local churches come under the protection of the Pope while continuing with their own non-Latin church life, but they are very much the exception rather than the rule, and the Roman hierarchy quickly decided that no such exception should be made in this case.

Many Anglican doubters still hoped that some kind of 'special case' could be made for them within the Roman Catholic Church, and many were deeply disappointed when the Roman Catholic bishops of England and Wales finally made their statement on the matter. They said, in effect, that each case would be treated on its own merits, and that individuals joining the Church would have to do so because they wanted to be Roman Catholics, not because they wanted to be Anglicans without women priests. Special consideration would, of course, be given to whole parishes joining the Roman Catholic Church from the Anglican Church, but they too would have to be received into the Roman Catholic Church; they could not just remain vaguely Anglican.

Furthermore, no promises could be made about whether or not Anglican priests could become priests in the Church of Rome. The bishops reiterated what has long been the traditional Roman Catholic position: that Anglican orders have no validity, so that in their eyes, Anglican priests are not actually priests at all. Certain Anglican priests who have gone over to Rome *have* been ordained as Roman Catholic priests, and some of those who are leaving over November 1992's decision (including some married men) seem to have been assured that they will be priested by individual Roman Catholic bishops, but the Roman hierarchy is not prepared to make a general statement to that effect.

This is partly because the matter is by no means straightforward for the Roman Church. Many prominent lay and ordained theologians in the Catholic Church quite openly support the ordination of women. What would happen to newly admitted Anglican-Roman priests if the Church of Rome decided to ordain women? Also, many Anglican priests are married, whereas Roman clergy are supposed to be celibate. The Roman hierarchy is already under considerable pressure on this point from those within their own Church who want to see the celibacy ruling abandoned. If they were to admit floods (if indeed we are talking about floods rather than trickles) of married Anglicans to the priesthood, it would be almost impossible to make a case for continuing to demand celibacy from 'real' Roman priests.

The Roman Catholic Church has also had to consider its relations with the Anglican Church. The Cardinal of Westminster, Archbishop Basil Hume, is reported to have said, after Synod's vote, that perhaps some of these developments signalled the 'conversion of England' – a deeply emotionally charged phrase for English Roman Catholics, for whom it would inevitably conjure up visions of the Roman priests martyred under Elizabeth I, pursuing a vision of a reunited church. Cardinal Hume seemed to be implying that the Church of England was in some sense not yet 'converted', and that the numbers leaving it would now be able to join the true Church.

He quickly backtracked on that, however, and the Roman Church has refused, officially, to take any line on the Church of England's decision at all, simply stating that to oppose the ordination of women was not in itself thought to be a sufficient reason for acceptance into the Roman Church. While correspondence between the present Pope and the previous Archbishop of Canterbury, Robert Runcie, makes it clear that the present Roman hierarchy regards the priesting of women as untraditional and a grave obstacle to unity, none the less the Roman Church is not constituted by its opposition to women priests, and is not prepared to accept such opposition as the only badge of membership from those who wish to be received.

Other options for opponents

So many of those who had hoped to be allowed to continue as some kind of 'Anglicans' under the patronage of the Pope are being forced to reconsider their position. They were almost certainly unrealistic in their expectations of Rome, but that does not mitigate their disappointment.

For those who are opposed to the priesting of women, who yet could not easily become Roman Catholics – and remember that this includes the majority of Evangelical opponents of the measure – the focus of attention shifted to what the Church of England was prepared to do to make their continuing membership a possibility. They were not eligible for financial recompense, since they were hoping not to have to leave, but what other kinds of recompense was the Church offering?

The legislation on which Synod voted did contain some measures to safeguard the position of those who opposed the measure. Many members of Synod who were actually in favour of women's ordination, or at least agnostic, were actually deeply dubious about the package on which Synod had to vote. They doubted that it was workable, or that it would even be acceptable to opponents of the measure. They have been proved very largely right by the months of negotiation that followed the vote. More than one member of Synod, on both sides of the debate, has wished that the vote was a straight question of whether or not women should be ordained, rather than a very contorted question about whether this was the legislation that would best carry the Church forward. One member said: 'We ought to have legislation less concerned about those who leave and more generous to the great majority of the opponents who would wish to stay . . . It would be administratively less tidy, pastorally sound, workable, hold us together and minimise secession'[19] – whereas the legislation on which Synod actually voted seemed actually to plan for schism. Opponents of November 1992's vote quickly pointed out that the legislation preserved their rights only for a very limited period, and that it did not take sufficient account of disagreement within a diocese.

The legislation assumes that bishops who are already in office, and who oppose the ordination of women, may refuse to allow any women priests to be ordained in their dioceses; or that, while allowing women priests to officiate, they may refuse to put them in charge of parishes; or may refuse a woman priest a licence to officiate. These refusals stand for the period of the bishop's ministry and for six months after a new bishop starts work in the diocese. The legislation also permits a local parish church to refuse the priestly or authoritative ministry of women, but not the ministry of women altogether. Congregations may refuse to accept a woman vicar to run their parish, and they may refuse to allow a woman to preside at the Eucharist.

What was not clear was what would happen in areas where a bishop who is in favour of women's ordination has large numbers of priests and parishioners who are opposed. It would then be a question not just of whether the ministry of a woman priest was acceptable, but whether the ministry of a bishop who had ordained women priests was acceptable.

In response to these objections, the bishops issued a statement in June 1993 (the Manchester Statement) setting out an immensely complicated scheme to ensure that no one need receive episcopal ministry from hands contaminated by ordaining women.

The scheme proposes that each region in the Church of England will have a 'regional' bishop, opposed to the ordination of women, who will carry out episcopal duties for such parishes and priests as are opposed to women's ordination. Such a bishop will act at the request of the diocesan bishop, not just whenever any dissenting priest or parish asks him; and, for preference, he will be a bishop from within the region, who already bears episcopal office.

But there will be some regions where the bishops are largely in favour of women priests, so that there is no obvious bishop to look after 'traditionalists'. To meet this need, the Archbishops of Canterbury and York will each appoint 'Provincial Episcopal Visitors'. These bishops, who will be suffragans – that is, assistant bishops without dioceses of their own – will supposedly work with local diocesan bishops and with the archbishops to ensure that opponents of women priests will have proper care.

This seems, at the time of writing, to be the scheme that the Church of England will actually adopt. The diocese of London is already putting a variation on this theme into operation. London has a diocesan bishop and several assistants, only one of whom is prepared to ordain women. Those opposed to women's ordination and those in favour will be 'serviced' by different assistant bishops, while theoretically all remain under the episcopal oversight of the diocesan bishop, David Hope. The 'London Plan' has been hailed as a pattern for other areas, in that it respects the opinions of opponents of women priests without making the whole of London a 'no-go' area for them.

It is not yet clear if this kind of compromise will be acceptable to all. The Manchester Statement has not met with universal approval from Cost of Conscience members. In particular, they are worried about the *continuing* care and provision for opponents of November's vote. Evidence from other countries where women have been ordained suggests that toleration of opponents of women priests is relatively short-lived, while Cost of Conscience believe that opposition will continue. They are therefore concerned that bishops opposed to women priests should continue to be appointed, and that systems of priestly and episcopal care for parishes who cannot accept women priests will also be permanent. In fact, they are beginning to press for this to be enshrined by parliamentary legislation, not just by the goodwill of synodical acts, which can be changed comparatively easily.

One paper put out by Cost of Conscience even advocates that 'there must be provision for the separate selection, training and ordination of opponent candidates [for the priesthood]', and that a new system of appointing bishops should be devised to ensure that bishops opposed to women's ordination continue to be appointed.[20] This statement makes it very clear how impossible the situation will actually be. What this writer is asking for is, in effect, a separate church.

One of the suggestions put forward by opponents of women's ordination was, in fact, that the Church of England should divide itself and create a new province. Within Britain at present, the Anglican churches in Wales, Scotland and Ireland are separate provinces. They run themselves financially and legislatively, they appoint and train their own clergy, and they are not bound by the decisions of General Synod. Supporters of the 'Third Province Movement' have suggested that England should add to its present two provinces of Canterbury and York a third, non-geographical province that would consist of those opposed to women's ordination. This would remain 'Anglican', as Wales, Ireland and Scotland are, but it would be able to run itself entirely without reference to the provinces that do ordain women. For all kinds of reasons, this proposal has not received much serious support. It would, of course, entail huge financial and legal problems in effecting a separation of property for the Third Province, and it would look, from the outside, like a much more serious split in the Church than the present scheme whereby opponents and supporters all still belong to the Church of England.

The Third Province Movement does, however, have the great merit of taking the position of *lay* opponents seriously.

They could be part of a church where they would be assured of sympathetic ministry. Other schemes tend to assume that priests and congregations are largely in accord, so they skate over hypothetical situations such as a parish priest being in favour of the ordination of women, but a large minority of parishioners being opposed. Do they have to receive a woman priest if the vicar invites her, or can they apply to a 'Provincial Episcopal Visitor' over his head? Or what happens if a parish priest is opposed, while most of his congregation are not? Are they to be deprived of women's priestly ministry on those grounds? In rural areas, where one Anglican priest officiates over several widely dispersed parishes, what are laypeople to do if their views do not coincide with those of their vicar? Most schemes tend to ignore these points, and assume that bishops and clergy can settle matters between them, and laypeople will be content with the end product. The Third Province idea does at least allow laypeople to continue in a church that is free of these ostensible sources of strife.

Theologically, too, the Third Province Movement has much to recommend it. It maintains the present understanding of episcopal and priestly ministry as centred in the local community, and it ensures the continuation of a ministry which, those who receive it may be sure, is 'apostolic' and untainted by women. If opponents of November's measure are in any serious doubt about whether women priests will come to be accepted throughout the universal Church, it is surely wise to maintain a branch of the Anglican Church that has never 'sullied' its ministry, so that there will be a source of 'pure' Anglicanism to return to.

From the point of view of women priests, too, this would have its advantages, since the province in which they then functioned could be wholeheartedly welcoming to their ministry. The two provinces could then exist side by side, and time would tell which one was the most effective. There is a wily Jewish politician in Acts, by the name of Gamaliel. In the story (Acts 6: 34–42), he favours leaving the Apostles to get on with things, rather than arresting them, on the sensible principle that if God is with them, they will succeed whatever the politicians do; and if not, then they will fail without intervention, too. The Third Province would allow a kind of Gamaliel principle to operate over women priests.

The Manchester Statement, on the other hand, entails all kinds of theological and practical anomalies. For one thing, who will consecrate these 'Provincial Episcopal Visitors'? Presumably, it would have to be only bishops who have not ordained women themselves, or the line becomes suspect. To whom do priests take their oath of canonical obedience? Legally speaking, it would have to be the diocesan bishop, even where a priest had no intention of letting the diocesan bishop ever darken the doors of his parish church. What happens if a diocesan bishop and a 'Visitor' bishop disagree about whether or not a certain parish has sufficient numbers of dissidents to need 'alternative episcopal oversight'? How can a bishop who believes that women *cannot* be priests allow a woman to administer what he would consider to be invalid sacraments to her congregation, even if he himself did not ordain her?[21] How are all these bishops actually *bishops* – that is, how do they stand in regard to the local church and the universal one? What happens if a bishop who is specifically ordained to minister to those opposed to women's ordination changes his mind?

These questions vary in importance, but there is a worrying degree of nebulousness about the matter. There is also a considerable amount of unwillingness to translate these arrangements into previously understood theological terms. What kind of episcopacy is this, and what kind of church-within-a-church? It is very hard to see how either side can actually be satisfied by these arrangements, and it is not yet clear whether opponents will, in fact, accept them and agree to try working along these lines.

What is remarkable is the amount of effort being put into maintaining these two apparently contradictory positions within one church. The sight of the Church's contortions has provoked incredulity among many on-lookers. And there have, indeed, been some bad moments – not least the sight of the bishops coming up with more and more plans to appease opponents, until it almost seems that they are saying that November's vote should not have happened; yet there is no certainty that the provisions will be acceptable to the majority of those who oppose women's ordination.

But the fact remains that many opponents of women's ordination still love the Anglican Church and wish to go on belonging to it, if they possibly can. In days gone by, women like Maude Royden had to go elsewhere to fulfil their calling. Geoffrey Kirk, a vociferous opponent of women's ordination, has suggested that they should continue to do just that – go and find some other (usually Protestant) church that would have them, in effect.[22] A great many women resisted that, because the Church of England belonged as much to them as to their opponents, and because it was to the priesthood of *this* church they were called, not just to priesthood in general.

The tables are now turned, and it is the opponents of women priests who are having to protest their loyalty to the Church of England and their certainty of belonging *here* and nowhere else, despite their painful sense of dispossession.

But it remains to be seen if the Church of England can actually find a coherent way to hold together women priests and those who oppose them. Even if it succeeds in the immediate future, long-term questions must remain about the continuing place of future generations of dissenters. If opponents of the ordination of women continue to make up about one-third of the Church of England in future generations, will that mean that the Church was wrong to ordain women? If the opposition dwindles, will their right to refuse women's priestly ministry still have to be protected? These are questions that must be faced at some time.

Many readers of this book will doubt that any provision should have been made for those who oppose Synod's decision. So much attention has been focused on the needs of opponents of the measure that there has been almost no chance to celebrate or plan for the very thing that the Church actually committed itself to. Indeed, some women deacons have actually reported a *rise* in hostility from previously unconcerned parishioners who have been able to read only the stories of those opposed to women priests. It is almost as though this great step of faith and hope is being subverted before it has even begun.

But in fact, it is important at least to attempt to make room for those who doubt whether women should be priests. By staying in the Church of England, however hesitantly and with whatever safeguards, they are committing themselves at least to the *possibility* that women priests are the will of God, otherwise they would surely have to leave this church altogether. Their continuing presence at least seems to leave a door ajar between the opposing factions.

It is important to keep in mind that the priesting of women does not introduce more *theological* diversity into the Church of England than it already had, since all the opinions held by those on both sides have been around for a long time. It certainly does, however, introduce more visible and practical disunity. In that sense, at least, opponents of November 1992's decision might claim a right to their sense of grievance against its supporters. It is our firm belief that just as its theological diversity has always been one of the strengths of Anglicanism, while making it impossibly difficult to administer tidily, so, too, this determination shown by both sides to go on belonging together, however impractical and even comical the means, will prove to be a transformative symbol of hope for other Christian churches, not just the tangled mishmash it may appear on the surface.

Postscript

THIS BOOK BEGAN with a celebration: the song of triumph that arose from the crowded pavement outside Church House when the result of the Synod vote was announced. *Jubilate Deo! Jubilate Deo!* But we seem to have ended on a more sober note, acknowledging the immense difficulties and uncertainty the Church of England now faces as it goes on to make the 'yes' vote a reality.

In fact, however, we believe that the picture is far from gloomy, and that even the tortuous horse-trading to keep the Church together discussed in Part III is actually part of the triumph song. Books will doubtless be written which survey the Christian past and its treatment of women and end with November 1992, but of course the vote is not the end. The Church has paid lip service to women before, notably when it voted that there were no 'theological objections' to their ordination. What makes this vote different is that the result must now be carried through, given flesh, made incarnate. The details of how this is to be done, how costly it is, in all ways and to all parties, seem to us to be the essential stuff of reality, and of holiness. The way in which God works in the world has to take into account the 'nuts and bolts', the real situations of real people, and although that is never easy, without it there can be no revolution.

But the slow process of giving flesh to the legislation enabling women to be priests is not the only cause for rejoicing. There are many other ways in which the 'yes' vote is already causing a sea-change in the mood of the Church of England.

The most important celebrations will be occurring in many dioceses up and down the country as this book appears: the celebrations in cathedrals and in parish halls as congregations welcome their newly ordained women priests. This, after all, is what it is all about – allowing women to serve the people by whom and for whom they feel called.

There is also a new mood of confidence in the 'catholic' wing of the Church among those who support women's ordination. Now that this piece of 'constitutional' business is out of the way, and 'catholic women priests' can join their brothers and sisters, lay and clerical, the catholic movement can turn its attention again to the great issues of social concern and of worship with which they have always been identified in the past. At a meeting in summer 1993 of a group called 'Affirming Catholicism', the renewed optimism and vigour of catholic Anglicans was almost tangible.

We would also like to pay tribute to many writers who have ensured that the funny side of this whole business is never forgotten. From inside the arena, there has been the satirical broadsheet, UPPITY, ever ready to poke fun at those who take themselves too seriously. And from outside, there have been disinterested commentators like Edward Pearce of the *Guardian*, who have reminded us just what a good *spectacle* the last few years of the Church of England's life have provided.[1] As Pearce himself weighed in with an article, he said, impishly: 'One makes no apology for joining in; it is far too good a fight.' All kinds of people have joined in on that basis. It is striking how few people are without an opinion on women priests, even those who have no church affiliation whatsoever. And some of them even go on to reassess Christianity in the light of this renewed attention, as Pearce himself does: 'One reason why we non-believers join the debate is that Christianity reaches far beyond narrow self-definition . . . This may be the after-breath of Christianity but, respectfully, that afterbreath is of more weight than the vengeful (and un-Christian) office politics for which [some opponents] now speak.'

And if the Church of England's debate has been of interest to non-believers, it has been of even more interest to many Roman Catholic observers who know that the issue of women's ministry cannot be avoided by Rome for ever. Some of those who rejoiced with their Anglican friends outside Church House in 1992 were Roman Catholic women, and they were there partly in solidarity and partly in hope. Many non-Anglicans believe that, in bringing the deep divisions about women so publicly and dramatically into the open, the Church of England has achieved something for all Christian churches. 'One cannot believe', writes the Roman Catholic author and journalist Margaret Hebblethwaite, 'that any other church will ever need to go through such a fuss again.'[2]

We cannot know for sure that she is right until the Roman Catholic Church does face up to this issue, but British Anglicans will test that hypothesis rather sooner: the Church in Wales and the Episcopal Church of Scotland will be voting on the priesting of women during 1994, and the 1992 vote in England says nothing about whether women priests can go on to become bishops, so it is possible that the spectacle will continue.

But one thing we do know is that for many people, the Synod vote in 1992 was a symbol of hope, a sign that the Church is indeed capable of conversion. Its conversion has been public and humiliating, and that has been part of its value. What other institution would be prepared to lay itself open like this? The Archbishop of Canterbury reminded Synod that this measure is really about 'enlarging the sympathies and generosity of our church in line with the generosity of God'.[3] And since the generosity of God is boundless, we can expect that the process of enlargement will go on for ever.

NOTES

Part I

1. The different ways in which women's groups approached this ban on women priests in the Church of England is discussed in Part II.
2. *The Ordination of Women to the Priesthood: The Synod Debate* (Church House Publishing, 1993), p. 26.
3. An 'illegal ordination' of eleven women took place in Philadelphia on 29 July 1974 before a congregation of over two thousand; a further three women were ordained in Washington the following winter. In terms of the Catholic theology of priesthood, upheld within the Anglican Communion in its official statements, these ordinations constituted an outrageous act of disobedience, but as Sara Maitland points out: 'In terms of the theology commonly accepted in the USA and in terms of the conscientious conviction of the women concerned they were both courageous and prophetic' (*A Map of the New Country: Women and Christianity* [Routledge & Kegan Paul, 1983]), p. 100. The position of all fifteen women was regularised after the 'yes' vote in 1976, though there can be no doubt that many felt that the Church's hand had been forced. See also Mary S. Donovan, *Women Priests in the Episcopal Church* (Forward Movement Publications, 1988) for further information; on page 26 there is a map that shows which dioceses still do not accept women priests.
4. This position is also held by Evangelical opponents of the measure. The Church Society, which has attempted to seek a judicial review to determine whether Synod was within its rights to allow women's ordination, says it stands for 'Bible, church and nation', see *Church Times*, 13 August 1993.

5.	See Brian Heeney, *The Women's Movement in the Church of England 1850–1930* (Oxford University Press, 1988), pp. 97–8.

6.	*The Synod Debate*, p. 75. The office of Reader dates from 1866. Readers are formally trained and licensed by a bishop to teach, preach, lead prayer, and assist the clergy in pastoral work. Women's admission to this office was therefore seen to conflict with teachings on 'headship'.

7.	ibid., p. 38.

8.	ibid., p. 28.

9.	Roman Catholics and Anglicans, for example, have different rulings on birth control, based on their interpretation of the 'proper' purpose of sex in marriage.

10.	*Synod Debate*, p. 42.

11.	See the New Testament story of the woman 'with the issue of blood' who touches Jesus and is healed. The shock of her action lies in the fact that an 'unclean' woman should not have touched a man at all (Mark 5: 24 ff.).

12.	Rosemary Radford Ruether, *Sexism and God-Talk* (Beacon Press, 1983), pp. 22–3.

13.	For example, Ephesians 5: 21–33.

14.	For example, 1 Timothy 2: 14.

15.	For excellent statements of these changed relationships, see Colin Craston, *Biblical Headship and the Ordination of Women* (Grove Books, 1986) and George Carey, in *Feminine in the Church*, ed. Monica Furlong (SPCK, 1984).

16.	Alec Graham, Bishop of Newcastle, *Synod Debate*, p. 41; Dr Avis, ibid., p. 40.

17.	The religious revival in early nineteenth-century Britain was spearheaded by Nonconformist churches. The Methodist Church, founded by John Wesley in the eighteenth century, became – and remains – a spiritual home for many people, particularly among the disenfranchised and unchurched urban poor. Christian feminism first arose in groups which defined themselves against the Anglo-Protestant, mainstream of the late eighteenth and early nineteenth centuries. Early Methodism, along with other sectarian churches, encouraged women to teach, preach, and take leadership roles within the community.

For further information about this important and, until recently, underresearched period of women's history, see Barbara Taylor, *Eve and the New Jerusalem: Socialism and Feminism in the Nineteenth Century* (Virago, 1983); Barbara Brown Zikmund, 'The Feminist Thrust of Sectarian Christianity', in R. R. Ruether and E. McLaughlin (eds), *Women of Spirit: Female Leadership in the Jewish and Christian Traditions* (Simon & Schuster, 1979), pp. 206–24.

18. Sara Maitland points this out in *A Map of the New Country*, p. 98: 'The acceptance of the Hong Kong ordinations by the rest of the Anglican Communion changed the situation more completely than most people are willing to recognise.' Certainly, since the first women were ordained in America in 1977, the matter has been part of the daily business of the Anglican communion.

19. Some parts of the Church, for example, are experimenting with 'locally ordained ministers', whose priesthood is, in theory, to be exercised only for the community for which they are ordained. Most theologies of the priesthood assume that a priest is ordained into the *universal* Church. This slight anomaly has caused remarkably little uproar – presumably because the 'local' priests are still men.

20. A number of different phrases are used in connection with this argument: 'icon of Christ', 'alter Christi', and so on.

21. E. L. Mascall, in *Man, Woman and Priesthood*, ed. Peter Moore (SPCK, 1978), p. 23.

22. *The Synod Debate*, p. 21.

23. For totally convincing proof of this, see R. Norris, in *Feminine in the Church*, pp. 71 ff.

24. C. S. Lewis, 'Priestesses in the Church?', in *God in the Dock: Essays on Theology*, ed. Walter Hooper (Fount Books, 1979).

25. The Reverend George Austen was quoted as saying that women priests would bring something 'wild' into Christianity. We don't think he meant it as a compliment (the *Guardian*, 12 November 1992).

26. This is a vast simplification of a complex position. For more details, see Peter Brown, *The Body and Society* (Faber & Faber, 1989), particularly Chapter 1.

27. For example, the martyrs Felicity and Perpetua, and the story about them in Sara Maitland, *Women Fly When Men Aren't Watching* (Virago, 1993).

28. Except, of course, by fundamentalists, who find it sufficient simply to quote the biblical texts. But as we have already argued (p. 14), this is not as straightforward as they would like to think.

29. See, for example, L. Boff, *The Maternal Face of God* (Collins, 1989). Boff suggests that the Holy Spirit is incarnate in the Virgin Mary, but unfortunately she shows her godhead by being meek and receptive, so although the book is theologically radical, it is not radical for women.

30. *Guardian*, 1 March 1993.

31. For a feminist theological assessment, see Henrietta Santer, in *Feminine in the Church*, pp. 139 ff.

32. P. Evdokimov, quoted in *What Will Happen to God?*, W. Oddie (SPCK, 1984), p. 70.

33. ibid., p. 12.

34. An obvious example of this is Tertullian, who wrote to women: 'You are the one who opened the door to the Devil', but also wrote of a wife: 'They pray together, they worship together . . . Where there are two together, there also He [Christ] is present.' Both quotes are taken from Eleanor McLaughlin, 'The Christian Past: Does It Hold a Future For Women?', *Anglican Theological Review*, January 1975, pp. 40–41.

Part II

1. Kate Millett, *Sexual Politics* (Virago, 1969), p. 128.

2. Given that, as we also suggest in Part I, the 'discoveries' of modern biblical scholarship have undermined scriptural arguments against this measure and against Christian feminism generally, it is worth noting the degree to which laypeople are still 'shielded' from the fruits of such inquiry: the pretext being that it might destroy their 'simple faith'. Church leaders like Bishop David Jenkins, who get into hot water for their 'agnosticism' about 'Christianity's central teachings', are, we submit – and he

maintains – doing no more than airing data and questions that are familiar to anyone who has been through theological studies.

3. *St Thérèse of Lisieux, Her Last Conversations*, trans. John Clark, OCD (ICS Publications, 1977), p. 260, quoted in *The Tablet*, 9 January 1993.

4. The same thing happened to women's ministries in the early nineteenth century (see Part I, Note 17). As new groups move from informal sects to organised churches, there is a tendency for the leadership to become professionalised and for women's role to be severely curtailed. The Methodist Conference, for example, barred women preachers in 1803.

5. It was an Oxford Movement (see p. 18ff) churchman, one Dr Pusey, who was a prime mover in founding and nurturing these new Anglican Sisterhoods, which made them deeply suspect not just for luring women from the hearth but as a dangerous form of 'Romanisation'.

6. Kathleen Bliss, *The Service and Status of Women in the Churches* (SCM Press, 1948). Dr Bliss condemned the 'influence' women had traditionally wielded in the churches: 'This is the form of power to which women, especially very able women, had been confined by their exclusion from responsible power.' She went on to suggest that the 'choice between influence and responsibility' was a crucial one facing both the Church and women themselves. By 1954 Dr Bliss's commission had evolved into a permanent department of the World Council of Churches, commonly known as the Women's Desk.

7. Personal correspondence, 1 June 1993.

8. It would not, in this context, be invidious to single out Professor Rosemary Radford Ruether's work as the earliest and most formative influence upon British Christian feminism. See her (edited) symposium *Religion and Sexism* (Simon & Schuster, 1974) and *New Woman New Earth: Sexist Ideologies and Human Liberation* (Seabury, 1975), both among the first US books on this topic to become widely available in the UK. Ruether has continued to contribute writings on this theme over the last twenty years. A frequent visitor to Britain, she has

consistently put her international status at the disposal of the movement here. Susan Dowell's own book, *Dispossessed Daughters of Eve: Faith and Feminism*, co-authored with Linda Hurcombe and published by SCM Press in 1981, was the first British offering to attract widespread attention. In 1983, Routledge & Kegan Paul (a mainstream 'secular' publishing house) brought out Sara Maitland's *A Map of the New Country*, which was researched and published on both sides of the Atlantic. The books quoted in this work represent a small cross-section of a growing list.

9. Elizabeth Canham, *Pilgrimage to Priesthood* (SPCK, 1983), p. 19.

10. Kath Burn, *The Calling of Kath Burn* (Angel Press, 1988), p. 12.

11. ibid., p. 81.

12. ibid., p. 80.

13. Personal correspondence, 1 February 1983. The closure of *Spare Rib*, announced as we were preparing this book, has led to a spate of further comparisons between the 'achievements' of US and UK feminism. Eileen Fairweather, once a *Spare Rib* worker, attributes the magazine's demise to its wilful alienation of the majority of its readers (*Guardian*, 15 March 1993). US feminist projects, like *MS.* magazine, continue to flourish but do so in a somewhat different context – one in which, as Ruether points out, feminism itself has not suffered from an imposed ghettoisation. On the same page (a week before on 8 March, International Women's Day) Catherine Bennett wrote bemoaning the lack of British 'star' feminist writers, and asking whether this too might be attributable to a certain 'will to fail' dourness among British feminists. One of Bennett's interviewees, however, the writer Ros Coward, distinguished some more positive features of UK feminism, and suggested that it was less 'simplistic' than its American counterpart: 'The feminism coming out of America is consistently that kind of radical feminism that is not attentive to issues of class, doesn't really care about general improvements other than in the most rhetorical sense.' The question of whether individual 'stardom'

weighs against or contributes to women's commonweal is a particularly pertinent one for Christian women now that some of us are being 'raised up' in a very particular symbolic way. As we hope is clear, we see a class-aware/left-wing suspicion of stardom as a positive contribution to feminism and the Church, one which is in no way narrow or humourless. We further propose that a socialist perspective, and the pre-eminently practical approach that has characterised feminist endeavour in this country, constitute a valuable offering to feminism worldwide, and a tradition which could be particularly useful to women in the USA, where feminism has sometimes overinvested in individual achievement at the expense of social critique.

14. Initiated by a Christian women's group in Oxford. See Angela West, 'Greenham Vigil – a Christian Women's Theological Initiative for Peace', *New Blackfriars*, March 1986. Sadly, the tendencies outlined above undermined the open-to-all policy which had made Greenham a unique site of *rapprochement* between different 'interest' groups of women.

15. Sara Maitland and Jo Garcia (eds), *Walking on the Water: Women Talk about Spirituality* (Virago, 1983), was the first non-fiction title to appear under feminist auspices. Marion Zimmer Bradley, *Mists of Avalon* (Sphere, 1984), a powerful evocation of female wisdom in Celtic religion, has been a popular bestseller.

16. Womanchurch Convergence, a network of mainly Roman Catholic feminists, which originated in the USA in the early 1980s. This group does not entirely dissociate itself from the mainstream but sees the need for autonomous communities for women's own theologising, ritual and worship. Rather than petitioning for change from the Church, Womanchurch stresses that women themselves *are* the Church. This can be a useful, radical and infinitely more realistic position for all kinds of women, particularly in a situation of near-complete intransigence on the part of the authorities. But when it precludes 'doing business' with authorities who are attempting to resolve questions of woman's place, perhaps it is not so radical.

17. Monica Furlong, 'Watersheds and Waterholes', *Feminist Theology*, 1, September 1992.

18. Lynne Segal, *Is the Future Female?: Troubled Thoughts on Contemporary Feminism* (Virago, 1987), p. 38.

19. Reported in *UPPITY* (a supporters' satirical newsletter), 7.

20. Emma Hebblethwaite, *Guardian* 17 November 1992.

21. Eleanor McLaughlin, 'Treasures Old and New', in S. Dowell (ed.), *One More Eve,* Christian Action Journal Spring 82, p. 18.

22. ibid., p. 17.

23. Penny Nairne, in *Chrysalis* (MOW's own journal), July 1993, p. 10.

24. Professor Charles Raven, referring to the same event (recorded in Acts 10–11) as Archbishop George Carey (p. 23). Cornelius was a Roman centurion who asked St Peter to baptise him. Peter resisted, but was told by God in a dream: 'What God has cleansed you must not call common' (Acts 11: 9). Peter baptised Cornelius, convinced that 'If then God gave the same gift to them as he gave to us when we believed in the Lord Jesus Christ, who was I that I could withstand God?' This has been a vital proof text for women's inclusion in all ministries of the Church.

25. Priests for the Ordination of Women was founded in the early 1980s, to convert fellow clergy.

26. *Faith in the City: A Call to Action by Church and Nation* (The Report of the Archbishop's Commission on Urban Priority Areas: Church House Publishing, 1985).

27. Just war teaching does not condemn outright taking up arms against an aggressor (which means it is a tradition that can be drawn upon by any of us who are not thoroughgoing pacifists). Nor is it the 'thin edge of the wedge' of Christian acquiescence in militarism, for it lays down stringent conditions which must be met before a war can be deemed 'just'. The Gulf War (and to some extent the Falklands War) was a 'classic' test case: it met many of the criteria: Saddam Hussein's aggression against Kuwait was a just cause; the war was declared by a proper authority (the UN); but it manifestly failed to meet the requirement of 'proportionality' – that the suffering caused must not outweigh that already perpetrated by the aggressor. For

details see the statement of the Christian Coalition for Peace in the Gulf, available from Christian CND and printed in full in *Church Times*, January 1991.

28. British Christians have given a good deal of thought to ways in which this theology can be applied to our own situation: for example, Terry Drummond and Mary Neave, *Liberation Theology and British Christians* (Jubilee Publications). (The Jubilee Group, a socialist/Christian network to which we both belong and whose name derives from Old Testament teaching on social justice, has produced a number of helpful publications in this whole area. For details and booklist contact Jubilee Group, 48 Northampton Road, Croydon CR0 7HT.)

29. *Faith in the City*, p. 50.

30. *The Kairos Report: A Theological Comment on the Political Crisis in South Africa*, published by the Catholic Institute for International Relations (22 Coleman's Fields, London N1 7AF: Third World Theology series) and the British Council of Churches (2 Eaton Gate, London SW1 9BL) in 1985 (quote taken from p. 15).

31. The Papal Encyclical *Pacem in Terris* (1963) states: 'Since women are becoming ever more conscious of their human dignity, they will not tolerate being treated as mere material instruments, but demand rights befitting a human person both in domestic and public life . . . Human beings have the right to choose freely the state of life which they prefer, and therefore a right to follow a vocation to the priesthood or religious life.'

32. *The Ordination of Women to the Priesthood: The Synod Debate* (Church House Publishing, 1993), pp. 62-3. Bishop Williamson was quoting Bishop John A. T. Robinson. (The audience were deeply moved by this speech, but it did not stop the next speaker from imputing Williamson's advocacy of this measure to 'our contemporary views of what may or may not be just': p. 63.)

33. For an up-to-date theologically focused account of ordained women in America, see Catherine M. Prelinger (ed.), *Episcopal Women: Gender, Spirituality and Commitment in an American Mainstream Denomination* (Oxford University Press, 1993).

34. Quoted in *Country Way*, a journal of 'Life and Faith in Rural Britain', Autumn 1992, p. 11.
35. One of the warmest tributes to the clergy's role in inner-city life appeared in *Marxism Today* (January 1986). Tony Moss wrote that 'their unique combination of theology and experience means they do not judge government strategy by the mortgage rate, taxation level or dividend returns as other influential groups are bound to do.'
36. Highly commended for its breadth and theological seriousness is Richard Holloway (ed.), *Who Needs Feminism? Male Responses to Sexism in the Church* (SPCK, 1991).
37. Anon., personal correspondence, by request.
38. McLaughlin, 'Treasures Old and New', p. 19.
39. Margaret Miles in Prelinger (ed.), *Episcopal Women*, p. 340.

Part III

1. Daphne Hampson, *Theology and Feminism* (Blackwell, 1990).
2. ibid., p. 4.
3. Hampson describes Liberation Theology in terms of an interest area: 'it is less dangerous . . . to reformulate subsidiary [i.e. political] questions within the tradition than to reconceive God' (ibid., p. 148). But one of the things that feminist theology, in particular, questions is whether this rigid line between 'systematic' theology and 'political' theology is valid. It is *precisely* feminists' examinations of 'political' questions about the place of women in Christianity that have paved the way for Hampson's 'systematic' questions. For further discussion of her very important book, see S. Dowell, *Feminist Review*, Summer 1991, pp. 95–100.
4. William Oddie, *What Will Happen to God?* (SPCK, 1984). By collapsing the entire spectrum of Christian feminism into the category of embittered militancy, Oddie demonstrates a seemingly wilful ignorance about feminism. Grist seems to be doing the same with Christianity. While

it is important to acknowledge that biblical religion absorbed many of the symbols of older goddess religions, its insistence upon monotheism – that is, a belief in one God, who is neither male nor female – represents a fundamental rejection of 'the goddess'. Grist's argument is essentially a restatement, in promotional terms, of Lewis's 'priestess' argument (see p. 25). (Tony Grist, *Guardian*, 20 February 1993.

5. It, is not uncommon for people (usually men) in these churches to claim that they have 'solved' the problem of religious sexism. Women ministers themselves tell a different story; see Mary Levinson, *Wrestling with the Church* (Arthur Jones, 1992). For further information on the status of women priests in the USA, see Mary S. Donovan, *Women Priests in the Episcopal Church* (Forward Movement Publications, 1988), particularly the figures on pp. 22–3.

6. Sara Maitland, *A Map of the New Country: Women and Christianity* (Routledge & Kegan Paul, 1983), p. 105.

7. ibid., p. 48.

8. Elizabeth Schussler Fiorenza, *Discipleship of Equals*, (SCM, 1993), p. 19.

9. ibid., pp. 23 ff.: 'Should women aim for ordination to the lowest rung of the hierarchical ladder?' Schussler Fiorenza was actually talking about ordination to the diaconate, since the article was originally written in 1967, but her arguments are pertinent to the present discussion as well.

10. See Mary Tanner, 'Called to Priesthood: Interpreting Women's Experience', in Monica Furlong (ed.), *Feminine in the Church* (SPCK, 1984). See also Monica Furlong's own useful article 'Watersheds and Waterholes', *Feminist Theology*, 1, September 1992, in which she distinguishes 'dark' and 'light' feminism, with their different concerns.

11. These quotes appear in an advertising feature presented by WAOW in *The Church Times*, 10 July 1982.

12. Ruth B. Edwards reports someone as saying 'that a female priesthood requires a second incarnation with Christ as a woman', *Scottish Journal of Theology*, vol. 46, no. 1, 1993, p. 122. She is reviewing *Man, Woman and Priesthood*, a book edited by J. Tolhurst.

13. Anne Widdecombe's speech to a Forward in Faith rally, London, 1 May 1993, reported in *The Tablet* of the same date.

14. Mary Gordon, *Good Boys and Dead Girls* (Penguin, 1991), p. 181. Lefebvre split with the Roman Catholic Church primarily over his insistence that the Mass should continue to be said only in Latin.

15. Monica Furlong, 'Watersheds and Waterholes', p. 85.

16. Bishop William Wantland, 'Conscience and Statute', *New Elizabethan Papers*, no. 4 (Cost of Conscience, 1993), p. 8.

17. Quoted by Wantland, ibid., p. 10. The statement is actually taken from a document produced by the Eames Commission, an inter-Anglican commission on the ordination of women.

18. *The Ordination of Women to the Priesthood: The Synod Debate* (Church House Publishing, 1992), p. 91.

19. Hugh Craig, ibid., p. 46.

20. Stephen Trott, 'Not Binding', Cost of Conscience, 1993, pp. 3–4.

21. This is a point made by the Reverend John Cruse in *The Church Times*, 16 July 1993. He writes: 'If the diocesan is convinced that women priests are an impossibility, even if he caters for his tender conscience by calling in one of the envisaged flying bishops to carry out his functions at the institution [of a woman priest to a parish], is he not committing those parishioners, for whom he is ultimately responsible, to receiving what he believes to be invalid sacraments?' (p. 11).

22. Geoffrey Kirk, *The Tablet*, 11 January 1992.

Postscript

1. Edward Pearce, the *Guardian*, 17 April 1993.
2. Margaret Hebblethwaite, *Guardian*, 28 November 1992.
3. *The Synod Debate*, p. 23.

Index

Santer, Henrietta, 122
Schussler Fiorenza Elizabeth,
    86, 129
Scott, Ted, 7
Segal, Lynne, 59, 126
Slavery see also Abolition, 20
St Hilda Community, 49, 55

Tanner, Mary, 129
Taylor, Barbara, 121
Teresa of Avila, 89
Teresa, Mother, 88
Tertullian, 122
Thatcher, Margaret, 15
Thérèse of Lisieux, 42, 88,
    123
Tractarians see also Oxford
    Movement, 17
Trott, Stephen, 130

UPPITY, 114, 126

Wantland, William, 97, 98, 99,
    130
WAOW (Women Against the
    Ordination of Women),
    87–90
Wesley, John, 120
West, Angela, 125
Widdecombe, Anne, 8, 92, 130
Wilberforce, William, 20
Williamson, Roy, 71, 127
WIT (Women in Theology), 49
Womanchurch, 58, 125
Woodforde, Parson, 19
World Council of Churches,
    46, 123

Zimmer Bradley, Marion, 125

DATE DUE			
FEB 2 4 1997			
MAR 3 1 1997			
APR 2 1 1997			
DEC 1 0			